P9-DEU-631

THE ULTIMATE
FOOTBALL
TRIVIA BOOK

THE ULTIMATE FOOTBALL TRIVIA BOOK

600 QUESTIONS
FOR THE SUPER-FAN

CHRISTOPHER PRICE

SPORTS
PUBLISHING

Copyright © 2019 by Christopher Price

All rights reserved. No part of this book may be reproduced in any manner without the express written consent of the publisher, except in the case of brief excerpts in critical reviews or articles. All inquiries should be addressed to Sports Publishing, 307 West 36th Street, 11th Floor, New York, NY 10018.

Sports Publishing books may be purchased in bulk at special discounts for sales promotion, corporate gifts, fund-raising, or educational purposes. Special editions can also be created to specifications. For details, contact the Special Sales Department, Sports Publishing, 307 West 36th Street, 11th Floor, New York, NY 10018 or sportspubbooks@skyhorsepublishing.com.

Sports Publishing® is a registered trademark of Skyhorse Publishing, Inc.®, a Delaware corporation.

Visit our website at www.sportspubbooks.com.

10 9 8 7 6

Library of Congress Cataloging-in-Publication Data is available on file.

Cover design by Tom Lau
Cover photo credits: Getty Images

Print ISBN: 978-1-68358-340-0
Ebook ISBN: 978-1-68358-341-7

Printed in the United States of America

This one is for Mr. Meschonat, my eighth-grade English teacher. He was the first grownup outside of my own family to say, "Hey, you know you could be a sportswriter." Thanks for helping me reach the right path.

Contents

Acknowledgments

The acknowledgments are always the most fun part of any book. No matter how solitary an endeavor book writing can be, it can't be done without the help of a lot of people, and this is my chance to thank all the people who helped make it a reality. First, as always, my thanks go out to super-agent Alec Shane, a guy who has helped jumpstart the second phase of my work as an author and always has my best interest at heart. Alec, you are the best—thank you for all that you do. Thanks to Julie Ganz at Skyhorse for helping this project see the light of day, and to Joseph Webb as fact-checker. It was a pleasure and honor to be able to work with the both of you.

Quite simply, I could not have completed this book without the gold mine that is Pro Football Reference. Their site is indispensable to me in my daily work, and it made the verification process for a project like this one that much easier. All of their reference sites are top notch. Go and visit them.

Been blessed to have come across plenty of terrific colleagues here, most of whom are too numerous to mention, but they include great and good friends who have provided support and encouragement along the way. Most have been thanked in previous editions, but I have to make sure I give a special shout-out to Stephen Popper and Georgia Churilla, two terrific friends. *Stephen and Georgia, everyone.*

It takes a village to write a book, and this is the ideal chance to thank everyone who is part of our community. The Starbucks on Washington Street in Wellesley is a great place to write for many reasons, including the fact that they don't skimp on the espresso shots. Our neighbors are terrific, and community friends help provide an amazing support system. But ultimately, it's all about family: Mom, Dad, Kelly, Jas, Molly, Marc, and Mina are as good a test audience as any author could ever hope for. And finally, my everlasting appreciation and love go out to Kate, Noah, and our faithful cat Stretch. They work hard to make sure I have the best home-field advantage in the world.

Introduction

Growing up, I was a sports geek.

I loved playing the games, sure. But when I saw my first real curveball when I was 11 years old or so, I realized my future was more in writing about sports than playing them. (I was more Ogilvie than Kelly Leak.) While I continued as an athlete—a growth spurt enabled me to play football and basketball later on—my love of writing fused with my love of sports. So I devoured pretty much everything I could get my hands on, and did as much reading and writing as I could. I joined the school newspaper, and I usually had one of these four things with me at all times: anything written by Zander Hollander, the *Baseball Encyclopedia*, *Sports Illustrated* (shout-out to Grandma and Grandpa Dunn for saving the old ones for me), and the *Boston Globe* sports page.

The upshot to all of it? Now, I get to live my dream. I've been a sportswriter all my professional life. It's all I ever wanted to do. While I've dabbled in other sports, I've been a football writer since 2001, having spent the better part of the last 18 years covering the Patriots. (My father was a minister, and in truth, I was always a little struck as to how similar our jobs were/are: We both have non-traditional vocations that don't fit into the 9-to-5 stereotype. We both work weekends, and the week always built to the big payoff. Every so often, we would have to try and soothe people in occasional times of travail. And we both engaged with people of deep faith and spoke to those who would look forward to salvation every Sunday.)

We tried to make this the sort of trivia book that's accessible to any and all football fans. As a result, even if you can't tell if a football is blown up or stuffed, there are questions in here that you'll still be able to figure out. And if you're a hardcore football fan, there are questions for you as well that will test your knowledge of the ultimate team sport. Along the way, I hope you guys have fun trying to figure it all out.

Anyway, this is a book for the kids who are growing up as sports geeks. There's no Zander Hollander anymore, but for the youngsters like me who love sports and history and stats and writing—and football—this is for you. I hope you enjoy it.

THE DRAFT

QUESTIONS

The first-ever NFL draft was held at the Ritz-Carlton in Philadelphia on February 8, 1936. (Prior to the inaugural draft, players were free to sign with any club.) With commissioner Bert Bell at the helm, it was a distinctly low-tech affair when compared to drafts of today. According to reports, there were 90 names written on a blackboard, and teams were basically told to *let 'er rip*. There were no scouting departments at that time, so teams pulled together lists from various media reports, visits to area colleges, and word of mouth between coaches, players, and league execs. It wasn't a wild success—in the end, just 24 of the 81 players drafted ended up signing with their new teams. (Four more ended up playing in 1937.) Among those not signing? First overall pick Jay Berwanger.

But the draft started to pick up steam, and it became the established method for restocking a team. While it was still a ways away from becoming the annual three-day event it is today, it grew and evolved throughout the 1940s and '50s, eventually expanding from nine rounds to 20. Teams started scouting departments in the 1940s, and those franchises started gaining separation from the rest of the league, forcing other teams to further develop their operations. One of the savviest owners in the early days was Wellington Mara of the Giants. Mara subscribed to several out-of-town papers and magazines in hopes of finding quality players, and the results could be seen on the field. After all, it wasn't a coincidence New York appeared in the NFL championship game eight times in 14 seasons (1933–47).

The draft moved from city to city throughout the '40s and '50s before settling in New York City in the 1960s, where it soon became a battleground for the feud between the AFL and NFL. The rival leagues held separate drafts from 1960 through 1966, before holding joint drafts from 1967–1969 prior to the merger. Post-merger, it was reduced from 17 rounds to a 12-round affair. In 1980, it was televised for the first time on ESPN; in 1988, ESPN and the NFL agreed to move it to the weekend, and TV ratings increased dramatically. Today, it runs seven rounds and has become a three-day televised spectacle of football, rotating from city to city so various fanbases can be a part of the circus.

GENERAL

1. In 1984, the NFL held a supplemental draft of players from the now defunct USFL. _____ was the first pick of that draft.
   Answer on page 37.

2. Which player DID NOT win a national championship in college and a Super Bowl title in back-to-back seasons?
   A. Cyrus Jones (Alabama, Patriots)
   B. William Floyd (Florida State, Niners)
   C. Tony Dorsett (Pitt, Cowboys)
   D. Marcus Allen (Southern Cal, Raiders)
   Answer on page 37.

3. True or False: Six Heisman Trophy winners have been taken first overall since 2000.
Answer on page 37.

4. True or False: No team has ever gone from the first overall pick to a Super Bowl win in the same season.
Answer on page 37.

5. These four teams have never had the first overall pick in the draft:
A. Broncos, Jaguars, Ravens, Seahawks
B. Broncos, Packers, Texans, Steelers
C. Niners, Seahawks, Patriots, Rams
D. Patriots, Steelers, Packers, Cowboys
Answer on page 37.

6. _____ and _____ are the two schools tied with the most first overall picks with five each.
Answer on page 37.

7. Match the position with the number of first overall selections

1. Offensive linemen	A.	17
2. Running back	B.	22
3. Defensive lineman	C.	35
4. Quarterback	D.	7
5. Wide receiver	E.	4

Answer on page 37.

8. Which former coach is responsible for the trade value chart that has been used as the gold standard throughout the league since the early 1990s?
A. Dave Wannstedt
B. Jimmy Johnson
C. Bill Cowher
D. Bill Parcells
Answer on page 37.

9. Of the years where players are eligible, which three drafts (not including the supplemental draft) are the only ones yet to produce a Hall of Famer?
Answer on page 37.

10. Name the seven No. 1 overall picks (not part of the supplemental draft) who have quarterbacked their teams to Super Bowl wins.
Answer on page 37.

11. Which team went 11 years—from 1969 to 1979—without a single first-round pick?
A. Washington
B. New York Giants
C. Philadelphia
D. San Francisco
Answer on page 37.

12. Which team ran out of time in 2003 when they were "on the clock" in the first round and ended up getting bumped down from seventh to ninth overall?
A. New York Jets
B. Washington

C. Seattle
D. Minnesota
Answer on page 38.

AFC EAST

Jets

1. Joe Namath was selected by both the AFL and the NFL in the 1964 draft. The Jets took him first overall. Which NFL team picked Namath, and where?
Answer on page 38.

2. Which one of these Jets draft picks was NOT a first-round selection?
A. Darrelle Revis
B. Keyshawn Johnson
C. Mark Gastineau
D. Al Toon
Answer on page 38.

3. How many quarterbacks were taken before Ken O'Brien in the first round of the 1983 draft?
Answer on page 38.

4. How many Heisman Trophy winners have played for the Jets?
Answer on page 38.

Patriots

1. Who was the Patriots' first overall pick in the 1982 draft?
Answer on page 38.

2. Tom Brady was drafted as the 199th overall pick in the 2000 NFL Draft. Do you know how many quarterbacks were taken before Brady, and who they are?
Answer on page 38.

3. Which quarterback was drafted first overall by the Patriots?
A. Steve Grogan
B. Doug Flutie
C. Scott Zolak
D. Jim Plunkett
Answer on page 38.

4. What did the Patriots trade to the Jets for the rights to hire Bill Belichick as head coach?
Answer on page 38.

Dolphins

1. Dan Marino was one of how many future Hall of Famers taken in the first round of the 1983 draft?
Answer on page 38.

2. How many quarterbacks have the Dolphins taken in the first round of the NFL draft?
Answer on page 39.

3. Hall of Famer Jason Taylor was taken in the third round out of Akron in which draft?
A. 1996
B. 1997
C. 1999
D. 2000
Answer on page 39.

4. Which one of the "Marks Brothers"—Duper or Clayton
—was taken earlier in the draft?
Answer on page 39.

Bills

1. How many times have the Bills taken Mr. Irrelevant?
   A. 3
   B. 4
   C. 5
   D. 0
   Answer on page 39.

2. How many University of Buffalo players have been drafted by the Bills?
   A. 0
   B. 1
   C. 2
   D. 3
   Answer on page 39.

3. Who was the first pick for the Bills in 1960, their inaugural draft?
   A. Richie Lucas
   B. Ernie Davis
   C. Carl Eller
   D. O. J. Simpson
   Answer on page 39.

4. Which former first-round pick of the Bills never played a down for the franchise?
A. Erik Flowers
B. Dan Marino
C. Haven Moses
D. Tom Cousineau
Answer on page 39.

AFC NORTH

Steelers

1. What year produced arguably the greatest draft in the history of the NFL—a draft where Pittsburgh selected Lynn Swann, Jack Lambert, John Stallworth, and Mike Webster in the same year?
A. 1970
B. 1971
C. 1968
D. 1974
Answer on page 39.

2. Only one Steelers quarterback was taken first overall. Who was he?
A. Ben Roethlisberger
B. Terry Bradshaw
C. Kordell Stewart
D. Cliff Stoudt
Answer on page 39.

3. True or False: Mean Joe Greene was the first overall pick in 1969.
Answer on page 39.

4. Who was the only running back taken before Le'Veon Bell in the 2013 draft?
A. Gio Bernard
B. Eddie Lacy
C. Montee Ball
D. Rex Burkhead
Answer on page 39.

Ravens

1. Who was the first player taken with the first pick in franchise history (1996)?
A. Jonathan Ogden
B. Ray Lewis
C. Peter Boulware
D. Ed Reed
Answer on page 39.

2. True or False: Michael Oher was taken with a higher overall pick than Ray Lewis.
Answer on page 39.

3. In franchise history, the Ravens have taken three quarterbacks in the first round of the draft. Name them.
Answer on page 40.

4. The Ravens have drafted more players from these two schools than any other college or university.
A. Miami and Boston College
B. Alabama and Oklahoma
C. Louisville and Texas
D. Maryland and Florida State
Answer on page 40.

Bengals

1. How many players who have been drafted by Cincinnati have gone on to the Hall of Fame?
A. Five
B. One
C. Ten
D. Four
Answer on page 40.

2. In their franchise history, the Bengals have selected a quarterback five times in the top 10 picks overall. Name them.
Answer on page 40.

3. Which Bengals running back was selected higher overall —Ki-Jana Carter, Ickey Woods, or Corey Dillon?
Answer on page 40.

4. True or False: Boomer Esiason was the first quarterback taken in the 1984 draft.
Answer on page 40.

Browns

1. Cleveland has had the first overall pick in the draft five times in franchise history. How many times have they taken a quarterback with that pick?
A. Five
B. Four
C. Three
D. Two
Answer on page 40.

2. In which position have the Browns invested more picks than any other since they returned in 1999?
   A. Offensive lineman
   B. Linebacker
   C. Running back
   D. Defensive back
   Answer on page 40.

3. Who was the first pick of the Browns when the franchise was restored in 1999?
   A. Tim Couch
   B. Bernie Kosar
   C. Drew Bledsoe
   D. Rick Mirer
   Answer on page 40.

4. True or False: When Bill Belichick was a head coach with the Browns (1991–95), the franchise used three draft picks on quarterbacks.
   Answer on page 40.

AFC SOUTH

Titans

1. Name the two players who have been taken first overall by the Titans/Oilers in franchise history:
   A. Earl Campbell, John Matuszak
   B. John Matuszak, Marcus Mariota
   C. Marcus Mariota, Steve McNair
   D. Steve McNair, Earl Campbell
   Answer on page 41.

2. How many quarterbacks have been taken in the first round by the Titans/Oilers in franchise history?
A. Six
B. One
C. Three
D. Five
Answer on page 41.

3. Who was the lowest drafted member of the franchise to reach the Hall of Fame?
A. DB Ken Houston
B. WR Steve Largent
C. WR Charlie Joiner
D. DE Elvin Bethea
Answer on page 41.

4. Which school has produced the most first-round picks in franchise history?
A. LSU
B. Oklahoma
C. Alabama
D. Texas
Answer on page 41.

Colts

1. Five of the seven first-overall choices in franchise history have been quarterbacks. Can you name all five?
Answer on page 41.

2. This future Hall of Famer was taken first overall by the Colts in 1983, but wouldn't play a snap for them.
Answer on page 41.

3. True or False: Reggie Wayne, who was selected by the Colts in the first round of the 2001 draft, leads the franchise in total games played.
   Answer on page 41.

4. Of these four quarterbacks, all drafted by the Colts, which threw for the most yards over his career?
   A. Jeff George
   B. Bert Jones
   C. Chris Chandler
   D. Jack Trudeau
   Answer on page 41.

Texans

1. Who was the first overall pick in Texans' franchise history?
   A. David Carr
   B. Andre Johnson
   C. Mario Williams
   D. J. J. Watt
   Answer on page 41.

2. What years did the Texans have the first overall pick?
   A. 2002, 2003, 2014
   B. 2002, 2006, 2015
   C. 2002, 2006, 2014
   D. 2007, 2013, 2014
   Answer on page 41.

3. True or False: The Texans have selected more players out of the University of Texas than any other school.
   Answer on page 41.

4. Name four of the eight quarterbacks drafted by the Texans.
   Answer on page 41.

Jaguars

1. True or False: The Jaguars have drafted multiple Hall of Fame players since the franchise started in 1995.
   Answer on page 42.

2. Which fourth-round pick of the Jaguars in the 1995 draft would be dealt three years after he was selected in a trade that ultimately got Jacksonville a first-round pick, one they would use to draft one of the most famous players in franchise history, Fred Taylor?
   A. Reggie Barlow
   B. Seth Payne
   C. Tony Brackens
   D. Rob Johnson
   Answer on page 42.

3. Which quarterback was a higher overall pick by Jacksonville—Blake Bortles or Byron Leftwich?
   Answer on page 42.

4. Which Jaguars draft pick has played the most career games?
   A. Fred Taylor
   B. Brad Meester
   C. Tony Boselli
   D. Mark Brunnell
   Answer on page 42.

AFC WEST

Broncos

1. Who was the first draft pick in the history of the franchise?
   A. Bob Gaiters
   B. Merlin Olsen
   C. Bob Hayes
   D. Haven Moses
   Answer on page 42.

2. The Broncos drafted several players who would go on to the Hall of Fame, but achieve their greatest success with teams OTHER than Denver. Which one of these players falls into this group?
   A. Rulon Jones
   B. Randy Gradishar
   C. Dick Butkus
   D. Lyle Alzado
   Answer on page 42.

3. These two quarterbacks were the only two ever DRAFTED by the Broncos to throw for more than 10,000 yards at the NFL level.
   A. Jay Cutler, Brian Griese
   B. Jay Cutler, Tommy Maddox
   C. Jay Cutler, Gary Kubiak
   D. Jay Cutler, Jake Plummer
   Answer on page 42.

4. Which Broncos draft pick set a franchise record for most carries in a season?
A. Terrell Davis (sixth round, 1995)
B. Clinton Portis (second round, 2002)
C. Mike Anderson (sixth round, 2000)
D. Floyd Little (first round, 1967)
Answer on page 42.

Chargers

1. Who was the first player chosen in the draft in franchise history?
A. QB Billy Kilmer
B. DT Ernie "Big Cat" Ladd
C. T Byron Bradfute
D. QB John Hadl
Answer on page 42.

2. True or False: Dan Fouts was a first-round pick of the Chargers in 1973.
Answer on page 42.

3. John Jefferson was the first-round pick of the Chargers in 1978. Where did the wide receiver go to college?
A. San Diego State
B. UCLA
C. Arizona State
D. Northwestern
Answer on page 43.

4. Who is the highest-drafted kicker in Chargers history?
A. Rolf Bernischke
B. Nick Novak
C. Nate Kaeding
D. Bill McClard
Answer on page 43.

Chiefs

1. Prior to Patrick Mahomes in the 2018 playoffs, who was the last quarterback drafted by the Chiefs to win a playoff game for Kansas City?
A. Todd Blackledge
B. Alex Smith
C. Len Dawson
D. None
Answer on page 43.

2. Who was the first quarterback drafted by the Chiefs who would throw for at least 50 touchdown passes in a Kansas City uniform?
A. Len Dawson
B. Mike Livingston
C. Todd Blackledge
D. Steve Fuller
Answer on page 43.

3. Which Chief was taken the earliest in the draft?
A. Tony Gonzalez
B. Patrick Mahomes
C. Christian Okoye
D. Dontari Poe
Answer on page 43.

4. Which two NFL legends were drafted by the Chiefs, but would go on to achieve their greatest success elsewhere?
A. Dick Butkus and Gayle Sayers
B. Roger Staubach and Gayle Sayers
C. Terry Bradshaw and John Elway
D. Roger Staubach and Dick Butkus
Answer on page 43.

Raiders

1. Name the two quarterbacks the Raiders took when they've had the first overall pick.
A. Roman Gabriel and JaMarcus Russell
B. Ken Stabler and Todd Marinovich
C. Derek Carr and JaMarcus Russell
D. Ken Stabler and Marc Wilson
Answer on page 43.

2. True or false: The Raiders have *never* drafted a Hall of Fame wide receiver.
Answer on page 43.

3. The Raiders have drafted four Heisman Trophy winners. Who was the Raiders' lowest drafted Heisman winner?
A. Billy Cannon
B. Jim Plunkett
C. Bo Jackson
D. Howie Long
Answer on page 43.

4. Which Hall of Fame running back taken in the first round by the Raiders in the 1982 draft threw for six regular-season touchdowns over the course of his career—more than six other quarterbacks selected by the Raiders?
A. Mark Van Eeghen
B. Napoleon Kaufman
C. Marcus Allen
D. Pete Banaszak
Answer on page 43.

NFC EAST

Giants

1. Who was the only running back drafted by the Giants to top 10,000 career rushing yards in the NFL?
A. Joe Morris
B. Frank Gifford
C. Ron Dayne
D. Tiki Barber
Answer on page 44.

2. Who was the only offensive skill position player drafted by the Giants to top 10,000 career receiving yards in the NFL?
A. Amani Toomer
B. Plaxico Burress
C. Frank Gifford
D. Don Maynard
Answer on page 44.

3. Of these four, which Giants draft pick has thrown the most career touchdown passes in the NFL heading into the 2019 season?
A. Jesse Palmer
B. Odell Beckham
C. Tom Landry
D. Ryan Nassib
Answer on page 44.

4. The Giants have drafted 13 Hall of Famers. Which one was chosen as part of the supplemental draft?
A. Lawrence Taylor
B. Tom Landry
C. Phil Simms
D. Gary Zimmerman
Answer on page 44.

Eagles

1. The Eagles have drafted three quarterbacks who have passed for more than 200 touchdowns in the regular season in the NFL. Donovan McNabb and Randall Cunningham are two of them. Who is the third?
A. Carson Wentz
B. Frank Tripucka
C. Sonny Jurgensen
D. A. J. Feeley
Answer on page 44.

2. A second-round pick of Philadelphia in 2009, he holds the Eagles' rookie rushing record with 637 yards in his first year in the NFL.
A. Bryce Brown

B. LeSean McCoy
C. Correll Buckhalter
D. Keith Byars
Answer on page 44.

3. He holds almost every rookie passing record in franchise history, including passing yards and touchdown passes.
A. Ron Jaworski
B. Carson Wentz
C. Randall Cunningham
D. Donovan McNabb.
Answer on page 44.

4. Which quarterback—who would go on to great success in Philadelphia over the course of his career—was *not* drafted by the Eagles?
A. Ron Jaworski
B. Nick Foles
C. Carson Wentz
D. Randall Cunningham
Answer on page 44.

Redskins

1. Which one of the following players was taken first overall by Washington?
A. LaVar Arrington
B. Heath Shuler
C. Harry Gilmer
D. Sammy Baugh
Answer on page 45.

2. True or False: Joe Theismann was originally drafted by the Redskins.
Answer on page 45.

3. In terms of overall selection, who is the only quarterback in Redskins franchise history to throw for more than 10,000 yards who was taken by Washington with a pick 175 or later?
A. Mark Rypien
B. Jason Campbell
C. Gus Frerotte
D. Patrick Ramsey
Answer on page 45.

4. Two of the top three all-time leaders in receiving yards in the regular season drafted by the Redskins are Hall of Famers (Art Monk, Charley Taylor). Who is the third one?
A. Frank Wycheck
B. Chris Cooley
C. Brian Mitchell
D. Keenan McCardell
Answer on page 45.

Cowboys

1. True or False: Troy Aikman was selected with one of the picks the Cowboys got from the Vikings in the legendary Herschel Walker trade.
Answer on page 45.

2. Prior to the historic Walker trade, which player did Dallas coach Jimmy Johnson propose dealing to Oakland for multiple draft picks?

A. Michael Irvin
B. Emmitt Smith
C. Russell Maryland
D. Danny White
Answer on page 45.

3. Russell Maryland and Troy Aikman were two of the three first overall picks made by the Cowboys. Name the third one:
A. Tony Dorsett
B. Michael Irvin
C. Too Tall Jones
D. Roger Staubach
Answer on page 45.

4. Name the two players drafted by the Cowboys who topped 100 career sacks.
A. Randy White and Too Tall Jones
B. DeMarcus Ware and Jim Jeffcoat
C. Leon Lett and Russell Maryland
D. Greg Ellis and Tony Tolbert
Answer on page 45.

NFC NORTH

Bears

1. Which Bears legend was drafted highest?
A. Dick Butkus
B. Walter Payton
C. Mike Ditka
D. Brian Urlacher
Answer on page 46.

2. True or False: Walter Payton was the only member of the 1975 NFL draft class to rush for more than 5,000 yards in his career.
Answer on page 46.

3. Which Bears assistant coach called William "The Refrigerator" Perry a "wasted" pick after he was taken in the first round of the 1985 draft?
A. Buddy Ryan
B. Mike Lavellie
C. Mike Ditka
D. Glen Cooper
Answer on page 46.

4. What school did record-breaking Chicago return man Devin Hester attend?
A. Miami
B. Florida
C. Florida State
D. Jacksonville
Answer on page 46.

Vikings

1. He was the only wide receiver taken before Randy Moss in the 1998 NFL draft.
A. Jerome Pathon
B. Kevin Dyson
C. Marcus Nash
D. Jacquez Green
Answer on page 46.

2. Which Hall of Fame linebacker was taken in the second round of the 1963 draft by the Vikings out of the University of Minnesota?
A. Carl Eller
B. Bobby Bell
C. Dick Butkus
D. Alan Page
Answer on page 46.

3. Which member of the Baseball Hall of Fame was chosen in the 17th round by the Vikings in the 1973 draft?
A. Boog Powell
B. Lou Brock
C. Dave Winfield
D. Willie Mays
Answer on page 46.

4. He's the only quarterback drafted by the Vikings who is in the top 10 in franchise history among players drafted in passing and rushing yards.
A. Daunte Culpepper
B. Tarvaris Jackson
C. Teddy Bridgewater
D. Frank Tarkenton
Answer on page 46.

Lions

1. Detroit took three receivers with its first-round pick in three straight years, from 2003–05. Who were they?
Answer on page 46.

2. Who was the running back taken first overall by the Lions in the 1980 draft out of Oklahoma?
A. Billy Sims
B. Barry Sanders
C. Bo Jackson
D. Marcus Dupree
Answer on page 47.

3. He passed for the fewest yards of any of the 10 quarterbacks the Lions have taken in the first round in the history of the franchise.
A. Chuck Long
B. John Rauch
C. John Hadl
D. Andre Ware
Answer on page 47.

4. True or False: The Lions have had the first pick in the draft four times in franchise history. They have used that pick on defensive players all four times.
Answer on page 47.

Packers

1. Who was the Packers' first-round pick in 1989 who was touted as "The Incredible Bulk" in a *Sports Illustrated* cover story, only to flame out once he reached the NFL?
A. Reggie White
B. Tony Mandarich
C. Najeh Davenport
D. B. J. Raji
Answer on page 47.

2. Of the quarterbacks drafted by the Packers, he's second
on the list of all-time passing yards at the NFL level.
A. Aaron Brooks
B. Daryle Lamonica
C. Mark Brunell
D. Matt Hasselbeck
Answer on page 47.

3. Which quarterback was taken ahead of Aaron Rodgers in
the 2005 draft?
A. Ben Roethlisberger
B. Eli Manning
C. Philip Rivers
D. Alex Smith
Answer on page 47.

4. Of this group, who was chosen highest in the draft by the
Packers?
A. Kicker Mason Crosby
B. Quarterback Bart Starr
C. Offensive lineman Jim Ringo
D. Quarterback Dan Majkowski
Answer on page 47.

NFC SOUTH

Saints

1. Who was the New Orleans coach when the franchise swapped virtually its entire draft class for the rights to select running back Ricky Williams?
   A. Mike Ditka
   B. Jim Mora
   C. Bum Phillips
   D. Sean Payton
   Answer on page 47.

2. True or False: Williams eventually rushed for more yards than any back ever drafted by the Saints.
   Answer on page 48.

3. True or False: In their franchise history, the Saints have drafted as many punters in the first round as quarterbacks.
   Answer on page 48.

4. Who was the lowest drafted player in New Orleans franchise history to make the Pro Football Hall of Fame?
   A. Morten Andersen
   B. Willie Roaf
   C. Rickey Jackson
   D. Archie Manning
   Answer on page 48.

Buccaneers

1. Tampa Bay's first-ever draft pick in franchise history was a defensive end who would go on to make the Hall of Fame. Who was he?

A. Lee Roy Selmon
B. Ricky Bell
C. Doug Williams
D. Hugh Green
Answer on page 48.

2. Lee Roy Selmon's brother was taken in the second round of that same 1976 draft. What was the name of the brother who was drafted?
A. Dewey Selmon
B. Lucious Selmon
C. Stevie Ray Selmon
D. Selmon Selmon
Answer on page 48.

3. What year did the Bucs use their two first-round draft picks—Nos. 12 and 28 overall—on a pair of defensive players who would end up in the Hall of Fame?
A. 2001
B. 1994
C. 1978
D. 1995
Answer on page 48.

4. True or False: Tampa Bay has had the first overall pick twice in franchise history. They have used that pick on a quarterback both times.
Answer on page 48.

Falcons

1. In which round did Atlanta take Brett Favre in the 1991 draft before trading him to Green Bay?
   A. First
   B. Second
   C. Third
   D. Fifth
   Answer on page 48.

2. The Falcons have had the first overall pick four times in franchise history. They've used two of those picks on linebackers. What are the other positions they've drafted when they've picked first?
   A. Wide receivers
   B. Cornerbacks
   C. Offensive linemen
   D. Quarterbacks
   Answer on page 48.

3. Jamal Anderson was one of the most productive running backs in Atlanta franchise history. Was he taken before or after wide receiver Bert Emanuel by the Falcons in the 1994 draft?
   Answer on page 49.

4. In franchise history, the Falcons have drafted three Hall of Famers. Favre and Deion Sanders are two of them. Who was the third?
   A. Claude Humphrey
   B. Steve Bartkowski
   C. Tim Mazzetti
   D. Tony Casillas
   Answer on page 49.

Panthers

1. True or False: The Panthers have never drafted anyone who has made the Hall of Fame.
   Answer on page 49.

2. This Heisman winner was selected in the fourth round by the Panthers out of Florida State in 2001, but because he had spent six years playing minor league baseball, he was the oldest player to ever receive the Heisman at age 28. Who was he?
   A. Steve Smith
   B. Kerry Collins
   C. Chris Weinke
   D. Tim Biakabutuka
   Answer on page 49.

3. Julius Peppers played football and _____ as a collegian at North Carolina before becoming the second overall pick of the Panthers in 2002.
   Answer on page 49.

4. True or False: Michael Reed—who was the "Mr. Irrelevant" of the 1995 draft—would go on to achieve a small measure of fame as one of the inventors of email.
   Answer on page 49.

NFC WEST

Seahawks

1. Which wide receiver was taken highest overall by Seattle?
   A. Joey Galloway
   B. Koren Robinson
   C. Brian Blades
   D. Golden Tate
   Answer on page 49.

2. True or False: Steve Largent was drafted by the Seahawks.
   Answer on page 49.

3. Five quarterbacks were taken before Seattle selected Russell Wilson 75th overall in the 2012 draft. Name them.
   Answer on page 49.

4. The Seahawks have had a top-5 pick seven times in their franchise history. Which one of these players was *not* taken with one of those choices?
   A. Earl Thomas
   B. Rick Mirer
   C. Cortez Kennedy
   D. Kenny Easley
   Answer on page 49.

Cardinals

1. These two players were taken with the first two choices in the 2004 draft ahead of Larry Fitzgerald, who went third overall to the Cardinals.
   Answer on page 49.

2. This Hall of Fame quarterback was taken in the 1965 draft by the Cardinals, but he decided to forsake the NFL for the AFL.
A. Charley Johnson
B. Joe Namath
C. Craig Morton
D. Jim Plunkett
Answer on page 49.

3. True or False: Dan Dierdorf was one of four future Hall of Famers taken in the first two rounds of the 1971 draft.
Answer on page 50.

4. This Arizona State product was the second-round pick of the Cardinals in 1997, but would go on to pass for more yards in the NFL than any draft pick in franchise history.
A. Jake Plummer
B. Neil Lomax
C. Josh McCown
D. Matt Leinart
Answer on page 50.

Niners

1. Eight quarterbacks who have been drafted by San Francisco have ended up throwing for 10,000 yards or more in the NFL. Name at least four of them.
Answer on page 50.

2. Who was the highest drafted running back (in terms of overall selection) in franchise history?
   A. Frank Gore
   B. Ricky Watters
   C. Roger Craig
   D. Ken Willard
   Answer on page 50.

3. This tight end out of Clemson was taken in the 10th round of the 1979 draft by San Francisco, but would go on to become one of Joe Montana's favorite targets.
   A. J. J. Stokes
   B. Dwight Clark
   C. Terrell Owens
   D. Russ Francis
   Answer on page 50.

4. This Hall of Famer was taken by the Niners after 11 other players at his same position in the 1996 draft out of Tennessee-Chattanooga.
   A. Terrell Owens
   B. Wesley Walls
   C. Dwight Clark
   D. Fred Dean
   Answer on page 50.

Rams

1. This Rams offensive lineman—taken in the third round of the 1976 draft by Los Angeles out of Jackson State—would go on to have a son who would win multiple Super Bowls as captain of the New England Patriots.
   A. Dick Bruschi

B. Rodney Johnson
C. Willie Law
D. Jackie Slater
Answer on page 50.

2. This quarterback, a fourth-round pick out of Nebraska in 1977, would go on to lead the Rams to an NFC championship in 1979.
   A. Dieter Brock
   B. Vince Ferragamo
   C. Jim Everett
   D. Pat Haden
   Answer on page 50.

3. The Rams traded second- and fifth-round picks to the Colts in the spring of 1999 for this running back.
   A. Jerome Bettis
   B. Marshall Faulk
   C. Edgerrin James
   D. Eric Dickerson
   Answer on page 50.

4. The Rams have had the first overall pick in the draft seven times. What position have they invested in the most when they've had their shot at the top of the draft?
   A. Running back
   B. Wide receiver
   C. Offensive tackle
   D. Quarterback
   Answer on page 50.

THE DRAFT

ANSWERS

GENERAL

1. Steve Young

2. D—Marcus Allen

3. True

4. True

5. A—Broncos, Jaguars, Ravens, Seahawks

6. Notre Dame and Southern Cal

7. 1-D, 2-B, 3-A, 4-C, 5-E

8. B—Jimmy Johnson

9. 1943, 1984, and 1992

10. Joe Namath, Terry Bradshaw, Jim Plunkett, Troy Aikman, John Elway, Peyton Manning, and Eli Manning.

11. A—George Allen loved wheeling and dealing. In that stretch, the closest the Redskins got was the 38th overall pick in 1971.

12. D—Minnesota. The Vikings were late that year and ended up taking defensive tackle Kevin Williams ninth instead of seventh.

AFC EAST

Jets

1. The St. Louis Cardinals took him 12th overall.

2. C—Mark Gastineau

3. 4

4. 3—John Huarte, Vinny Testaverde, Tim Tebow

Patriots

1. Kenneth Sims

2. 6:
   Rd. 1, Pick 18: Chad Pennington, NY Jets
   Rd. 3, Pick 65: Giovanni Carmazzi, SF 49ers
   Rd. 3, Pick 75: Chris Redman, Bal. Ravens
   Rd. 5, Pick 163: Tee Martin, Pitts. Steelers
   Rd. 6, Pick 168: Marc Bulger, NO Saints
   Rd. 6, Pick 183: Spergon Wynn, Cle. Browns

3. D—Jim Plunkett

4. On January 27, 2000, New England traded three draft picks, including a 2000 first-rounder, for two Jets picks and the rights to hire Belichick.

Dolphins

1. 7—John Elway, Eric Dickerson, Bruce Matthews, Jim Kelly, Richard Dent, and Darrell Green.

2. 4—Marino, Ryan Tannehill, Bob Griese, Rick Norton.

3. B—1997

4. Duper. He was taken in the second round in 1982, while Clayton was selected in the eighth round of the 1983 draft.

Bills

1. D—None

2. B—one player, wide receiver Drew Haddad, a seventh-round pick in 2000

3. A—Lucas, out of Penn State.

4. D—Tom Cousineau

AFC NORTH

Steelers

1. D—1974

2. B—Terry Bradshaw

3. False—he was taken fourth overall in 1969. The Bills selected O. J. Simpson first overall that year.

4. A—Bell was selected 48th overall, while Bernard was taken 37th.

Ravens

1. A—Jonathan Ogden

2. True. Oher was taken 23rd overall in the 2009 draft, while Lewis was selected with the 26th overall choice in the 1996 draft.

3. Joe Flacco, Kyle Boller, and Lamar Jackson.

4. B. They've drafted 11 players from Alabama and 11 from Oklahoma.

Bengals

1. B—One. Anthony Muñoz in 1980.

2. David Klingler, Greg Cook, Akili Smith, Jack Thompson, and Carson Palmer. (Wayne Peace and Clint Longley were top 10 picks of Cincinnati in the supplemental drafts of 1984 and 1974, respectively.)

3. Carter was taken first overall in 1995, while Woods was selected 31st in 1988 and Dillon was chosen 43rd overall in 1997.

4. True. Esiason was selected with the 38th overall pick that year.

Browns

1. Three—Baker Mayfield, Tim Couch, and Bobby Garrett. (For what it's worth, Bernie Kosar was the first overall pick of the Browns in the 1985 supplemental draft.)

2. D—Cleveland has drafted 39 defensive backs since 1999.

3. A—Tim Couch

4. False: He only drafted two quarterbacks in his tenure with the Browns—Eric Zeier in the third round of the 1995 draft and Keithen McCant in the 12th round of the 1992 draft.

AFC SOUTH

Titans

1. A—Earl Campbell and John Matuszak

2. A—Marcus Mariota, Vince Young, Steve McNair, Jim Everett, Dan Pastorini, and Jake Locker.

3. A—Houston was taken in the ninth round of the 1967 draft.

4. D—Five Longhorns have been taken in first round by the Titans/Oilers.

Colts

1. George Shaw, 1955; John Elway, 1983; Jeff George, 1990; Peyton Manning, 1998; Andrew Luck, 2012.

2. John Elway, who was traded to the Broncos.

3. True.

4. C—Chris Chandler with 28,484 yards.

Texans

1. A—David Carr

2. C—2002, 2006, and 2014.

3. False. The Texans have only taken five players out of the University of Texas.

4. David Carr, Deshaun Watson, Dave Ragone, Tom Savage, T. J. Yates, Drew Henson, Alex Brink, and B. J. Symons.

41

Jaguars

1. False—In their franchise history, they have never drafted a Hall of Famer.

2. D—Rob Johnson

3. Bortles was taken third overall in 2014, while Leftwich was selected seventh overall in 2003.

4. B—Meester. The second-round pick in 2000 played 209 career games.

AFC WEST

Broncos

1. A—Gaiters was the first choice of the Broncos in 1961.

2. C—Butkus was chosen by Denver in the second round of the 1965 draft out of Illinois near the height of the AFL-NFL feud, but would go on to star for the Bears for the duration of his career.

3. A—Cutler ended up with 35,133 career passing yards and Griese had 19,440.

4. A—Davis had 392 rushing attempts in 1998.

Chargers

1. C—Bradfute was taken in the 1960 AFL Draft by the Chargers.

2. False—Fouts was taken in the third round that year out of Oregon. Five quarterbacks were taken ahead of him—Bert Jones, Gary Huff, Ron Jaworski, Gary Keithley, and Joe Ferguson.

3. C—Arizona State

4. D—McClard was taken in the third round with the 61st overall pick out of Arkansas in the 1972 draft.

Chiefs

1. D—None. Mahomes was the first quarterback ever drafted by the franchise to win a playoff game.

2. B—Livingston, who was taken in the second round of the 1968 draft by Kansas City, threw for 56 career touchdowns while with the Chiefs.

3. B—Mahomes was chosen 10th overall in the 2017 draft.

4. B—Staubach was taken in 1964 and Sayers was taken in 1965, but both decided to play for the NFL instead of the AFL.

Raiders

1. A—Gabriel was the first overall pick of the Raiders in 1962, and Russell was the top selection in 2007.

2. False—The Raiders took Lance Alworth in the second round of the 1962 AFL draft, Fred Biletnikoff in the second round out of Florida State in 1965, and Tim Brown in the first round out of Notre Dame in 1988.

3. C—Jackson. He was selected as the No. 1 overall pick in the 1986 NFL Draft, but Jackson initially chose baseball. However, in 1987, Jackson's rights were returned to the draft, where he was selected by the Raiders in the seventh round. They worked out a deal where he could play both.

4. C—Allen, who also had 282 career passing yards.

NFC EAST

Giants

1. D—Barber. The second-round pick in 1997 out of Virginia ended his career with 10,449 regular-season rushing yards.

2. D—Maynard was a ninth-round pick of the Giants out of UTEP in 1957. He only played one year with the Giants before joining the Jets of the AFL and becoming Joe Namath's favorite receiver.

3. A—Palmer, a fourth-round pick in the 2001 draft out of Florida, threw three career touchdown passes. A former contestant on "The Bachelor," he's gone on to a lucrative second career on television.

4. D—Zimmerman. The offensive lineman out of Oregon was one of a handful of players who initially signed with the USFL, but were made available after the fledgling league folded. Those players were part of a supplemental draft, and Zimmerman's rights eventually bounced from the Giants to the Vikings.

Eagles

1. C—Jurgensen was taken in the fourth round of the 1957 draft out of Duke, and threw for 255 career touchdown passes in his career.

2. B—McCoy

3. B—Wentz rewrote the rookie passing record book in his first season with the Eagles.

4. A—Jaworski, who would take the Eagles to the Super Bowl in 1980, was a second-round pick of the Rams in 1973.

Redskins

1. C—Gilmer. The quarterback was chosen first overall in 1948 out of Alabama.

2. False: Theismann was initially drafted by the Dolphins in 1971, but after contract talks failed, he went to the CFL. The Redskins obtained his rights in 1974.

3. C—Frerotte was selected No. 197 overall in the 1994 draft out of Tulsa, but would go on to throw for 21,291 yards over the course of his NFL career.

4. D—Among players drafted by Washington, McCardell—a 12th-round choice out of UNLV in 1991—finished his pro career with 11,373 receiving yards.

Cowboys

1. False. Aikman was a first-round pick of the Cowboys before the deal.

2. A. Johnson initially thought about shipping Irvin to Oakland, only to reportedly be talked out of the trade by Raiders owner Al Davis.

3. C. Jones was the first overall selection in the 1974 draft out of Tennessee State.

4. B. Ware was taken in the first round of the 2005 draft out of Troy, and had 138.5 career sacks, while Jeffcoat was chosen in the first round of the 1983 draft out of Arizona State, and ended up with 102.5 career sacks.

NFC NORTH

Bears

1. A—Butkus was taken third overall in the 1965 draft out of Illinois.

2. True

3. A—Buddy Ryan

4. A—Hester was a second-round pick out of "The U" by the Bears in 2006.

Vikings

1. B—Dyson was taken 16th overall by the Titans and finished his career with 178 catches for 2,325 yards and 18 touchdowns. Moss was chosen 21st by the Vikings, and had 982 catches, 15,292 yards, and 156 touchdowns.

2. B—Bell was taken 16th overall by the Vikings in the 1963 draft. However, he would end up choosing the AFL, and played 12 seasons with the Chiefs.

3. C—Winfield never played college football, but was one of a handful of individuals who ended up being drafted in three professional sports—baseball, basketball, and football.

4. D—Tarkenton. He's first in overall passing yards with 47,003 and 10th in rushing yards at 3,674.

Lions

1. Charles Rogers, 2003; Roy Williams, 2004; Mike Williams, 2005.

2. A—Sims rushed for 5,106 yards in five seasons in the NFL.

3. B—Rauch was taken second in the 1949 draft out of Georgia, but passed for just 959 yards in his three years in the NFL.

4. False: They have used all four picks on offensive players—offensive end Leon Hart, running back Billy Sims, running back Frankie Sinkwich, and quarterback Matthew Stafford.

Packers

1. B—Mandarich never reached expectations, and was released after three-plus seasons with Green Bay. He was the only player taken in the top 5 of the 1989 draft not to make the Hall of Fame.

2. D—Hasselbeck, who was taken in the sixth round of the 1998 draft, ended up playing the bulk of his career with the Seahawks, and finished second to Aaron Rodgers when you compile his career passing yardage.

3. D—Smith was taken first overall that year by the Niners, while Rodgers was selected 24th overall, near the end of the first round, by Green Bay.

4. C—Ringo was chosen 80th overall in the 1953 draft by Green Bay.

NFC SOUTH

Saints

1. A—Ditka. The Saints offered their first-round, third-round, fourth-round, fifth-round, sixth-round, and seventh-round picks in the 1999 draft and their first-round and third-round picks from the 2000 draft to Washington for the fifth overall pick of the 1999 draft.

2. True. After struggling in his early years with New Orleans, Williams would go on to rush for 10,009 career yards. He ended up playing seven seasons in Miami and one with Baltimore.

3. True. New Orleans has taken one quarterback—Archie Manning—and one punter—Russell Erxleben—in the first round.

4. A—Andersen was chosen in the fourth round of the 1982 draft out of Michigan State.

Buccaneers

1. A—Selmon. The defensive end out of Oklahoma would go on to be inducted into the Hall of Fame in 1995.

2. A—Dewey, Lee Roy's brother, was taken in the second round that year by Tampa Bay. The third Selmon brother, Lucious, played with them collegiately at Oklahoma, but was drafted two years before by New England.

3. D—That year, Tampa picked Warren Sapp at No. 12 and Derrick Brooks at No. 28. Both ended up making the Hall of Fame.

4. False. Tampa Bay has picked first overall five times.

Falcons

1. B—Favre was selected 33rd overall out of Southern Miss.

2. D—Quarterbacks. The Falcons have taken linebackers Tommy Nobis and Aundray Bruce first overall, and have also selected quarterbacks Steve Bartkowski and Michael Vick in that same spot.

3. After. Emanuel was selected in the second round that year, while Anderson was taken in the seventh round.

4. A—Humphrey. The defensive end was a first-round pick of the Falcons in 1968 out of Tennessee State.

Panthers

1. True

2. C—Weinke was 29 as a rookie in 2001 with the Panthers.

3. Basketball

4. False

NFC WEST

Seahawks

1. A—Galloway was taken eighth overall in the 1995 draft.

2. False—Largent was drafted by the Oilers in the fourth round of the 1976 draft, but was dealt to Seattle prior to the season for an eighth-round pick.

3. Andrew Luck, Robert Griffin, Ryan Tannehill, Brandon Weeden, and Brock Osweiler.

4. A—Thomas was taken with the 14th overall choice in the 2010 draft out of Texas.

Cardinals

1. Eli Manning and Robert Gallery.

2. B—Namath was chosen 12th overall by the Cardinals, but decided to take his shot with the Jets and the AFL.

3. True—Dierdorf was taken with the 43rd overall choice in the 1971 draft by the Cardinals out of Michigan. Jack Ham, Jack Youngblood, and John Riggins were the other three.

4. A—Plummer would pass for 29,253 yards in the NFL with the Cardinals and Broncos.

Niners

1. Joe Montana, Alex Smith, Y. A. Tittle, John Brodie, Earl Morrall, Billy Kilmer, Elvis Grbac, Colin Kaepernick.

2. D—Willard was taken with the second overall pick in the 1965 draft out of North Carolina, and one of just three picks the Niners have made with the second overall selection.

3. B—Clark ended up catching 506 passes for the Niners over a nine-year career in the NFL.

4. A—Terrell Owens

Rams

1. D—Slater. His son Matthew has won three Super Bowls with the Patriots.

2. B—Ferragamo would lead the Rams to Super Bowl XIV, where they dropped a 31–19 decision to the Steelers.

3. B—Faulk was reportedly upset with his deal and looking to renegotiate, but ended up being shipped to St. Louis.

4. D—The Rams have taken four quarterbacks with the No. 1 pick—Billy Wade in 1952, Terry Baker in 1963, Sam Bradford in 2010, and Jared Goff in 2016.

ROOKIES

QUESTIONS

"They have no idea what they're getting into. It's not their fault. We all had to go through it at some point or another. They're going to get a big dose of what they probably haven't had a whole lot of certainly any time recently. It's a big load. The competition level is going to step up. The volume is going to step up."—Bill Belichick on rookies

"I want to rush for 1,000 or 1,500 yards. Whichever comes first."

—George Rogers, who was taken first overall in the 1980 draft by the Saints.

When it comes to life in the NFL, rookies don't have it easy.

In many cases, when they reach professional football, they're thrown into the deep end of the pool and told to swim. It's not like college, where there are redshirt years, and teams carry 100 players, and your season ends in November. You're no longer at the top of the mountain—instead, you're starting at the bottom, all over again. You go from being an All-American to a place where the wisest course of action is keeping your eyes and ears open and your mouth closed. It's a business, where players can be cut at the drop of a hat. The game is faster and more unforgiving, and the season lasts year-round. But for those who survive the cauldron that is the first year of the NFL, a standout rookie season can lead to bigger and better things down the road. In this chapter, we're going to examine some of the greatest rookie seasons in NFL history, and those who may have stumbled along the way.

OFFENSE

1. Eighteen quarterbacks have started all 16 regular season games as rookies. Name them.
   Answer on page 67.

2. Of that group of 18, two of them weren't necessarily "true" rookies. Name them and explain their circumstances.
   Answer on page 67.

3. Of that group of 18, who had the highest passer rating as a rookie?
   A. Cam Newton
   B. Russell Wilson
   C. Carson Wentz
   D. Dak Prescott
   Answer on page 67.

4. Three quarterbacks in that group of 18 tied for the most losses sustained by a rookie quarterback. Who were they?
   Answer on page 67.

5. Who is the only rookie quarterback to rush for more than 700 yards and 10 touchdowns?
   A. Cam Newton
   B. Michael Vick

C. Lamar Jackson
D. Andrew Luck
Answer on page 68.

6. Which one of these players *never* won the official Offensive Rookie of the Year award determined by the NFL?
A. Percy Harvin
B. Odell Beckham, Jr.
C. Larry Fitzgerald, Jr.
D. Keenan Allen
Answer on page 68.

7. Which rookie running back set the NFL record for most rushing yards in a season for a first-year player?
A. Eric Dickerson
B. Saquon Barkley
C. Jim Brown
D. O. J. Simpson
Answer on page 68.

8. Which rookie quarterback set the NFL record for most touchdowns in a season by a first-year quarterback?
A. Russell Wilson
B. Peyton Manning
C. Baker Mayfield
D. Ben Roethlisberger
Answer on page 68.

9. Which team has had the most AP Offensive Rookie of the Year winners?
A. Dallas
B. New England
C. Detroit
D. Minnesota
Answer on page 68.

10. In 1998, this rookie receiver set a then-NFL record for the most touchdown receptions by a rookie with 17, tops in the NFL that season.
A. Randy Moss
B. Antonio Freeman
C. Terrell Owens
D. Keyshawn Johnson
Answer on page 68.

11. This rookie quarterback became the first player in the history of the NFL to lead the league in both yards per attempt as a passer (minimum 350 pass attempts) and yards per attempt as a rusher (minimum 100 carries) in the same season.
A. Cam Newton
B. Michael Vick
C. Andrew Luck
D. Robert Griffin III
Answer on page 68.

12. Has a rookie quarterback ever won the Super Bowl?
Answer on page 68.

13. In 1937, Sammy Baugh had one of the most dominant rookie seasons of all time, leading the league in virtually every major passing category. He played other positions as well. What position did he NOT play?

A. Linebacker

B. Punter

C. Defensive Back

D. Quarterback

Answer on page 68.

14. This rookie running back made the first start of his career in Super Bowl XXII and set a Super Bowl rushing record.

A. Timmy Smith

B. Clarence Davis

C. Michael Pittman

D. Yancey Thigpen

Answer on page 68.

15. _____ was the only first-year player in NFL history to win AP Rookie of the Year and MVP in the same season.

Answer on page 68.

16. True or False: Dan Marino started Week One of his rookie year in the NFL.

Answer on page 68.

17. This rookie topped 1,000 receiving yards in his first year in the league, becoming the first tight end in NFL history to break through that mark.

A. Rob Gronkowski

B. Kellen Winslow

C. Mike Ditka

D. Tony Gonzalez

Answer on page 68.

18. Three rookie running backs have finished their first year in the NFL with 2,000-plus yards from scrimmage. Who were they?
Answer on page 69.

19. This future legend—who had a father and brother who also played in the NFL—struggled in his rookie year under center, throwing 28 picks in his first year in the league, a record for a rookie quarterback. Who was it?
Answer on page 69.

20. This Philly quarterback set the NFL record for most completed passes as a rookie.
A. Donovan McNabb
B. Carson Wentz
C. Ron Jaworski
D. Nick Foles
Answer on page 69.

21. Eight quarterbacks won 10 or more games as starters in their rookie year. Name them.
Answer on page 69.

22. Not all first-year signal-callers have success—five of them have lost 13 or more games in their rookie year. Name them.
Answer on page 69.

23. With the understanding that targets have only "officially" been counted as a statistic since 1992, _____ is the only pass catcher to top 100 catches and 160 targets in his rookie year in the NFL.

A. Anquan Boldin
B. Larry Fitzgerald
C. Odell Beckham
D. Terry Glenn
Answer on page 69.

24. The only two rookies to ever go for 20-plus touchdowns in their first year in the league played the same position. What was it?
Answer on page 69.

25. This rookie set the rookie league record for most all-purpose yards from scrimmage.
A. Eric Dickerson
B. Marshall Faulk
C. Tim Brown
D. LaDainian Tomlinson
Answer on page 69.

DEFENSE

1. Which one of these players *never* won Defensive Rookie of the Year?
A. Ndamukong Suh
B. Brian Cushing
C. Clay Matthews III
D. Kendrell Bell
Answer on page 69.

2. True or False: J. J. Watt was the only player ever to win Defensive Rookie of the Year and Defensive Player of the Year honors in the same season.
Answer on page 69.

3. This rookie defensive end led the league in sacks in 1999, notching one of the great debut seasons for any defender in recent NFL history.
A. Reggie White
B. Jevon Kearse
C. Derrick Thomas
D. Bruce Smith
Answer on page 69.

4. However, it is worth mentioning the NFL did not officially recognize sacks as an official stat until 1982. Before that, a Detroit defensive end had 23 in 1978 as a rookie. Who was it?
Answer on page 69.

5. Which rookie cornerback set a single-season record for interceptions that still stands?
A. Deion Sanders
B. Jalen Ramsey
C. Darrell Green
D. Dick Lane
Answer on page 70.

6. This linebacker set an NFL mark for most solo tackles as a rookie.
A. Patrick Willis
B. Jerod Mayo
C. Rickey Jackson
D. Chris Spielman
Answer on page 70.

7. In 1969, this rookie was part of a team that finished 1–13, but he ended up capturing Defensive Rookie of the Year honors and setting the table for a dominant run throughout the 1970s.
A. Elvin Bethea
B. Mean Joe Greene
C. Mel Blount
D. Randy White
Answer on page 70.

8. Which defensive lineman was taken second in the 2010 draft, but would go on to win the Defensive Rookie of the Year after compiling 10 sacks in his first year in the league?
A. Gerald McCoy
B. Ndamukong Suh
C. Jadeveon Clowney
D. Sheldon Richardson
Answer on page 70.

9. Name the rookie who finished his first year with a whopping 12 interceptions.
A. Deion Sanders
B. Ty Law
C. Darrelle Revis
D. Paul Krause
Answer on page 70.

10. These three players are all tied at the top of the list for most pick-sixes in their rookie year with three.
Answer on page 70.

11. This safety had one of the best rookie seasons of any defender in Chicago history, as he forced 15 turnovers as a rookie.
A. Richard Dent
B. Dan Hampton
C. Shaun Gayle
D. Mark Carrier
Answer on page 70.

12. Name the two teams that have had the most Defensive Rookies of the Year. HINT—They're both in the AFC.
Answer on page 70.

13. Since 2002, four Defensive Rookies of the Year have been suspended at some point for running afoul of league policy on either performance-enhancing drugs or substance abuse. Name them.
Answer on page 70.

14. This defender holds the record for most quarterback hits in a season by a rookie. (Information only available from 2006 to present.)
A. J. J. Watt
B. Clay Matthews
C. Von Miller
D. Aldon Smith
Answer on page 70.

15. Which Minnesota defensive lineman set the NFL rookie record for most fumbles recovered in a season with nine?
A. Jared Allen
B. Alan Page

C. Don Hultz

D. John Randle

Answer on page 70.

16. What did Art Tait do in his first year with the Giants that hasn't been done since by a rookie?

A. Returned two fumbles for touchdowns

B. Registered three safeties in one game

C. Tackled his own quarterback twice

D. Played all 11 defensive positions in one game

Answer on page 71.

17. Who was the only Defensive Rookie of the Year to go on to become a head coach in the NFL?

A. Jim Haslett

B. Robert Brazile

C. Lem Barney

D. Chip Banks

Answer on page 71.

18. One year, the Defensive Rookie of the Year Award was given to two players on the same team. What team did they play for?

A. Green Bay

B. Dallas

C. Atlanta

D. Pittsburgh

Answer on page 71.

19. Who is the only rookie in NFL history to finish his first season with at least four sacks, four interceptions, and at least 10 tackles for loss?

A. Lawrence Taylor

B. Lofa Tatupu

C. Steve Nelson

D. Brian Cushing

Answer on page 71.

20. In 2008, Baltimore's Jameel McClain did something as a rookie that had only been done one other time in league history by a first-year player. What was it?

A. Block two punts in one game

B. Score two defensive touchdowns in a game

C. Finish the year with two safeties

D. Recover two fumbles in one game

Answer on page 71.

21. This future Hall of Famer finished his rookie year with the Patriots as the only first-year player in NFL history with at least two punt returns for a touchdown and eight interceptions.

A. Ty Law

B. Lawyer Milloy

C. Tim Fox

D. Mike Haynes

Answer on page 71.

22. This defender was drafted at the age of 19—the youngest drafted player in NFL history—and played his rookie year with the Texans at the age of 20.

A. Tremaine Edmunds

B. Bruce Smith
C. Amobi Okoye
D. Tre'Davious White
Answer on page 71.

23. Who was the only rookie defender to finish his first year in the NFL with more than 10 sacks and 100 or more tackles?
A. Brian Urlacher
B. Jerod Mayo
C. Reggie White
D. Jevon Kearse
Answer on page 71.

24. Who was the last player to win Defensive Rookie of the Year and a Super Bowl ring in the same season?
A. Lawrence Taylor
B. Jack Lambert
C. Terrell Suggs
D. Dana Stubblefield
Answer on page 71.

25. According to multiple reports, this Falcons rookie finished his first year in the league with a whopping 294 tackles, an unofficial league mark for rookies.
A. Tommy Nobis
B. Jessie Tuggle
C. Keith Brooking
D. Stoney Case
Answer on page 71.

SPECIAL TEAMS

1. As a rookie, this player scored seven touchdowns, all on returns on either kicks or punts.
A. Deion Sanders
B. Devin Hester
C. Billy "White Shoes" Johnson
D. Cordarrelle Patterson
Answer on page 71.

2. Which rookie kicker posted 132 points in his first year, put together a perfect postseason run (hitting all 20 kicks, both field goals and extra points), and ended up as a Super Bowl champion and first-team All-Pro?
A. Justin Tucker
B. Adam Vinatieri
C. Stephen Gostkowski
D. Mike Vanderjagt
Answer on page 72.

3. In his first season in the league, rookie punter Steve Broussard did something just one other player in NFL history accomplished. What was it?
A. Had the ball snapped over his head multiple times
B. Punted a ball into the stands
C. Had three punts blocked
D. Punted the ball backward over his head
Answer on page 72.

4. This native Australian set an NFL rookie record for the best punting average (minimum 75 attempts).
A. Michael Dickson
B. Shane Lechler

C. Bryan Anger

D. Ryan Allen

Answer on page 72.

5. What first-year player holds the rookie record for most combined punt and kick return yards in league history?

A. Steve Smith

B. Darren Sproles

C. Stump Mitchell

D. Danny Amendola

Answer on page 72.

ROOKIES

ANSWERS

OFFENSE

1. Warren Moon (Houston), Jim Kelly (Buffalo), Rick Mirer (Seattle), Peyton Manning (Indianapolis), David Carr (Houston), Matt Ryan (Atlanta), Joe Flacco (Baltimore), Sam Bradford (St. Louis), Cam Newton (Carolina), Andy Dalton (Cincinnati), Russell Wilson (Seattle), Ryan Tannehill (Miami), Andrew Luck (Indianapolis), Geno Smith (New York Jets), Derek Carr (Oakland), Jameis Winston (Tampa Bay), Carson Wentz (Philadelphia), Dak Prescott (Dallas).

2. Moon was a 28-year-old who was in his first year in the NFL after spending six seasons in the CFL. Kelly was 26 after spending two years in the USFL with Houston.

3. D—Prescott finished his rookie year with a 104.9 passer rating. For what it's worth, he was also at the helm for 13 wins, tied for the most for any rookie quarterback in the history of the league. (Ben Roethlisberger went 13–0 in his rookie season after Tommy Maddox was injured.)

4. Warren Moon, Peyton Manning, and Derek Carr.

5. A—In 2011, Newton finished with 706 rushing yards and 14 touchdowns.

6. C—Fitzgerald

7. A—Dickerson had 1,808 rushing yards as a rookie in 1983. At the time, it was the sixth-highest single-season rushing total of all time.

8. C—Mayfield did it with Cleveland in 2018.

9. D—Chuck Foreman, Sammy White, Randy Moss, Adrian Peterson, and Percy Harvin all captured the honor while with Minnesota.

10. A—Moss had the most touchdown catches in the league that year. He led the league in that category five times during his career.

11. D—Griffin turned the trick with the Redskins in 2012.

12. No. There have been signal-callers in their first full year as starters who were almost rookies—like Tom Brady in 2001. But no rookie quarterback has ever won a Super Bowl, much less reached the big game.

13. A—In addition to playing quarterback, he also punted and played defensive back later in his career.

14. A—Smith ran for 204 yards in Washington's 42–10 win over Denver.

15. Jim Brown won the AP MVP and Rookie of the Year in 1957.

16. False: Marino took over in Week Six from David Woodley.

17. C—Ditka did it in 1961 with the Bears.

18. Eric Dickerson had 2,212 yards in 1983, Edgerrin James had 2,139 in 1999, and Saquon Barkley registered 2,028 in 2018.

19. Peyton Manning, who tossed 28 interceptions as a rookie with the Colts in 1998.

20. B—Wentz completed 379 passes in 2016, his first year in the NFL.

21. Dak Prescott, Ben Roethlisberger, Dieter Brock, Joe Flacco, Andrew Luck, Matt Ryan, Russell Wilson, Kyle Orton.

22. DeShone Kizer, Chris Weinke, Derek Carr, Peyton Manning, Warren Moon.

23. A—As a rookie, Boldin had 101 catches on 165 targets with the Cardinals in 2003.

24. Running back—Gayle Sayers had 22 with the Bears in 1965, and Eric Dickerson finished the 1983 season with 20 touchdowns with the Rams.

25. C—Brown had 2,317 all-purpose yards as a rookie with the Raiders in 1988.

DEFENSE

1. C—The linebacker with the Packers and Rams didn't take home the hardware.

2. False—It was Lawrence Taylor.

3. B—Kearse had 14.5 sacks that year for Tennessee.

4. Al "Bubba" Baker, whose season was highlighted by a memorable five-sack game against Tampa Bay.

5. D—"Night Train" had 14 picks for the Rams as a rookie in 1952.

6. D—Spielman finished the 1988 season with 153 tackles with the Lions, according to Pro Football Reference.

7. B—Greene won DROY honors that season and became the heart of Pittsburgh's Steel Curtain defense, helping lead the Steelers to four Super Bowl titles.

8. B—Suh was so dominant in his first season he was named by the players as the 51st-best player in the league in a players' poll after his rookie year.

9. D—Krause had 12 picks in 1964 with Washington and was named First-Team All-Pro as a result. He finished his career with 81 career interceptions.

10. Lem Barney did it with the Lions in 1967, Ronnie Lott had three with the Niners in 1981, and Janoris Jenkins—as a member of the Rams—made it a threesome in 2012.

11. D—Carrier forced 15 turnovers in 1990—10 interceptions and five forced fumbles.

12. The Jets and Chiefs have had four each. New York had Erik McMillan, Hugh Douglas, Jonathan Vilma, and Sheldon Richardson, while Kansas City has seen Bill Maas, Derrick Thomas, Dale Carter, and Marcus Peters take the honor.

13. Brian Cushing, Shawne Merriman, Sheldon Richardson, and Julius Peppers.

14. C—Miller had 29 quarterback hits with Denver in 2011, his first year in the league.

15. C—Hultz recovered an amazing nine fumbles in 1963 with the Vikings in his rookie year.

16. A. He returned a pair of fumbles that season for touchdowns; he's the only first-year player in league history to have ever done it.

17. A—Haslett, who won the award in 1979 with Buffalo, would go on to play linebacker for the Bills and Jets. He would serve as the head coach in New Orleans from 2000 through 2005, and serve as the interim head coach with the Rams in 2008.

18. C—Falcons teammates Buddy Curry and Al Richardson shared the award.

19. D—Cushing did it in his first season as a member of the Texans in 2009.

20. C—McClain and Jim Young—who was a rookie on the Oilers in 1977—each finished their rookie years with a pair of safeties.

21. D—Haynes, who was chosen in the first round of the 1976 draft, had eight picks and a pair of punt returns for touchdown that year for New England.

22. C—Okoye was taken in the first round of the 2007 draft.

23. C—In his first year with the Eagles, White had 100 tackles and finished with 13 sacks in just 13 games.

24. B—Lambert did it as a member of the 1974 Steelers.

25. A—Nobis. In 1966, Nobis was taken first overall by the expansion Falcons, and played 11 seasons for Atlanta.

SPECIAL TEAMS

1. B—Hester. As a rookie in 2006, Hester took back three punts for touchdowns and scored twice on kickoffs. He returned a missed field goal 108 yards for the longest touchdown in NFL history. And he returned the opening kickoff of the Super Bowl 92 yards for a score.

2. A—Tucker did it all in 2012, his first year with the Ravens.

3. C—Broussard, who was with the Packers at the start of the 1975 season, punted nine times in a game against the Lions and had three of them blocked. It's only happened one other time in NFL history.

4. A—Dickson averaged 48.19 yards per punt in 2018, his first year with the Seahawks.

5. D—As a rookie with the Rams in 2009, Amendola finished with a combined 1,978 yards on kick and punt returns.

PLAYERS

QUESTIONS

"It's not the X's and O's, but the Jimmy's and Joe's."
—unknown
"The achievements of an organization are the results of the combined effort of each individual."
—Vince Lombardi

I've always thought that if a player was lucky, there were three phases to his career. His rookie year, where he's just trying to keep his head above water as he tries to figure out a way to survive. The next two to three years, where you finally get the hang of what's going on at the NFL level, and if you're lucky enough, you get to stick around, and maybe even get a taste of some success. And the third level? That's usually reserved for the guys who have it all figured out—the lucky ones who have managed to scratch and climb their way to the top of the mountain. This section focuses on those who have reached the second and third phases of their careers—the guys who make up the heart of the NFL. There are all sorts of players who make it, and while I'll never dismiss anyone who even manages to realize their dream by playing a single snap in the NFL, this section celebrates those who have made it—those who make the magic we get to see every Sunday. (Or Monday . . . or Thursday . . .)

1. Who was the first to record 7 sacks in a single game?
A. Lawrence Taylor
B. Reggie White
C. Michael Strahan
D. Derrick Thomas
Answer on page 89.

2. Who has the league record for most official sacks in a season?
A. Bruce Smith
B. Brian Orakpo
C. Andre Tippett
D. Michael Strahan
Answer on page 89.

3. Who has the record for most consecutive games with a sack?
A. Bruce Smith
B. Kevin Greene
C. John Randle
D. Chris Jones
Answer on page 89.

4. This hard-luck quarterback holds the record for being sacked the most times in a 16-game season.
A. Deshaun Watson
B. Steve Spurrier
C. David Carr
D. Michael Vick
Answer on page 89.

5. This fearsome pass rusher was the first to incorporate the head slap into his repertoire, a move that was eventually banned.
A. Deacon Jones
B. Merlin Olsen
C. Bruce Smith
D. Bubba Baker
Answer on page 89.

6. This quarterback would go on to win multiple Super Bowls, but was sacked more than any other signal-caller in NFL history.
A. Peyton Manning
B. Ben Roethlisberger
C. John Elway
D. Brett Favre
Answer on page 89.

7. Which one of the following players did *not* return six kickoffs for a touchdown in his career?
A. Ollie Matson
B. Gale Sayers
C. Travis Williams
D. Deion Sanders
Answer on page 89.

8. Name the Patriots wide receiver who would go on to become a Super Bowl MVP who ended up playing some defensive back for New England early in his professional career.
Answer on page 89.

9. This former Chargers running back set the league record for most points in a season by a non-kicker.
Answer on page 89.

10. Who has the NFL record for most touchdowns in a career?
A. Jerry Rice
B. Emmitt Smith
C. Marcus Allen
D. Gayle Sayers
Answer on page 90.

11. Patriots quarterback _____ holds the NFL mark for most pass attempts in a game without an interception.
Answer on page 90.

12. Who holds the NFL record for most regular-season games played?
A. George Blanda
B. Morten Andersen
C. Adam Vinatieri
D. Jerry Rice
Answer on page 90.

13. What player holds the mark for most consecutive starts on defense?
A. Reggie White
B. London Fletcher
C. Bill Romanowski
D. Jim Marshall
Answer on page 90.

14. Which quarterback has two separate streaks of at least 100 consecutive regular-season starts or more?
A. Brett Favre
B. Eli Manning
C. Tom Brady
D. Philip Rivers
Answer on page 90.

15. Who has the record for most punting yards in NFL history?
A. Jeff Feagles
B. Sean Landeta
C. Shane Lechler
D. Rich Camarillo
Answer on page 90.

16. Who is the only punter in NFL history to go more than 1,000 consecutive punts without having one blocked?
Answer on page 90.

17. Sammy Baugh, Danny White, and Tom Tupa all shared this common characteristic when it came to much of their playing careers.
Answer on page 90.

18. _____ played the most seasons in NFL history.
Answer on page 90.

19. This former Bronco holds the NFL mark for most all-purpose yards gained in a single game.
A. Haven Moses
B. Terrell Davis
C. Rod Smith
D. Glyn Milburn
Answer on page 90.

20. Jerry Rice is first on the all-time list of most career yards gained from scrimmage. Who is second?
A. Emmitt Smith
B. Walter Payton
C. Randy Moss
D. Terrell Owens
Answer on page 90.

21. Who was the tallest player in the history of professional football?
A. Ed "Too Tall" Jones
B. Fred Dean
C. Charles Haley
D. Richard Sligh
Answer on page 90.

22. Who was the shortest player in the history of professional football?
A. Darren Sproles
B. Jack "Soupy" Shapiro
C. Mini Mack Herron
D. Dion Lewis
Answer on page 91.

23. Who was the youngest player to play in a game in NFL history?

A. Wes Welker

B. Gayle Sayers

C. Pat Mahomes

D. Amobi Okoye

Answer on page 91.

24. Who was the oldest player to take a snap in the NFL?

A. Tom Brady

B. George Blanda

C. Steve DeBerg

D. Adam Vinatieri

Answer on page 91.

25. Match the player with the team with which he *finished* his NFL career:

1. O. J. Simpson	A. Chargers
2. Jerry Rice	B. Niners
3. Johnny Unitas	C. Broncos
4. Franco Harris	D. Chiefs
5. Joe Montana	E. Seahawks
6. Emmitt Smith	F. Bears
7. Ricky Williams	G. Panthers
8. Reggie White	H. Ravens
9. Jared Allen	I. Cardinals
10. Ed Reed	J. Jets

Answer on page 91.

DOUBLE-DIPPING

1. A handful of stars over the years have doubled up, playing professional football and baseball along the way. See if you can match up these football players with the most notable baseball team they played for.

   1. Brian Jordan   A. Braves
   2. Deion Sanders   B. Mets
   3. Drew Henson   C. Royals
   4. Bo Jackson   D. Cardinals
   5. D. J. Dozier   E. Yankees

   Answer on page 91.

FANTASTIC FEUDS

Occasionally, players end up chirping at other players. Sometimes, it's with their teammates. And a lot of times, that'll end up with some fisticuffs, or at least some quality trash-talking. Here are our favorite feuds; we'll give you one name from the rivalry, you fill in the rest.

1. Terrell Owens
   Answer on page 91.

2. Darrelle Revis
   Answer on page 91.

3. Josh Norman
   Answer on page 92.

4. Richard Sherman, Part One
   Answer on page 92.

5. Richard Sherman, Part Two
   Answer on page 92.

6. Aqib Talib, Part One
   Answer on page 92.

7. Aqib Talib, Part Two
   Answer on page 92.

8. Tom Brady
   Answer on page 93.

9. Bill Bergey
   Answer on page 93.

10. Joe Montana
    Answer on page 93.

CANADIAN CLUBBERS

A handful of players have enjoyed success north of the border before reaching the National Football League. Below is the name of the player; name which CFL team they starred for north of the border.

1. Doug Flutie
   Answer on page 93.

2. Warren Moon
   Answer on page 93.

3. Cameron Wake
   Answer on page 94.

4. Rocket Ismail
   Answer on page 94.

5. Joe Theismann
   Answer on page 94.

6. Joe Kapp
   Answer on page 94.

7. Cookie Gilchrist
   Answer on page 94.

8. Mervyn Fernandez
   Answer on page 94.

9. Ed George
   Answer on page 94.

10. Harald Hasselbach
    Answer on page 95.

CFL-RELATED BONUS QUESTION

1. Who is the only player in the history of professional football to have won an XFL championship, a Super Bowl, and a Grey Cup?
   A. Warren Moon
   B. Doug Flutie
   C. Joe Theismann
   D. Bobby Singh
   Answer on page 95.

REMEMBERING THE USFL

The United States Football League was a short-lived circuit that ran for three years and mounted a (relatively) brief challenge to the NFL. Regardless, several stars made their mark in that span.

1. Which quarterback holds the record for most passing yards in a single game?
   A. Doug Flutie
   B. Jim Kelly
   C. Doug Williams
   D. Chuck Fusina
   Answer on page 95.

2. Which running back holds the mark for most rushing yards in a single game?
   Answer on page 95.

3. Two USFL teams played the longest professional football game in history—a triple-overtime playoff game in 1984. Which two franchises were involved, and who won?
   Answer on page 95.

4. Which franchise moved every year of the USFL's existence?
   A. Gamblers
   B. Express
   C. Breakers
   D. Generals
   Answer on page 95.

5. Of the original 12 teams in the 1983 USFL season, which two teams never made any of the USFL playoffs (1983–1985) before either the team folded or the league folded?
   Answer on page 95.

6. Name the four Heisman winners the USFL signed in its three years of existence.
   Answer on page 95.

7. Which franchise won the most games (playoffs included) in league history?

A. Philadelphia/Baltimore Stars

B. Tampa Bay Bandits

C. Los Angeles Express

D. New Jersey Generals

Answer on page 95.

8. Which quarterback started his career with the LA Express, but would go on to bigger and better things in the NFL, eventually landing in the Hall of Fame?

A. Joe Montana

B. Steve Young

C. Jim Kelly

D. Randall Cunningham

Answer on page 96.

9. Which running back won the USFL MVP in the league's inaugural season?

A. Herschel Walker

B. Kelvin Bryant

C. Chuck Fusina

D. Marcus Dupree

Answer on page 96.

10. Who was the first draft pick in USFL history?

A. Dan Marino

B. Jim Kelly

C. Herschel Walker

D. Doug Flutie

Answer on page 96.

11. Which USFL team drafted Jerry Rice?
A. Birmingham
B. New Jersey
C. Los Angeles
D. Houston
Answer on page 96.

12. Who was the all-time winningest coach in USFL history?
A. Steve Spurrier
B. George Allen
C. Walt Michaels
D. Jim Mora
Answer on page 96.

13. Match the player with his USFL team
1. Reggie White   A. Houston
2. Jim Kelly   B. Pittsburgh
3. Mike Rozier   C. Los Angeles
4. Brian Sipe   D. Memphis
5. Steve Young   E. New Jersey/Jacksonville
Answer on page 96.

14. Who was the longest-tenured commissioner in USFL history?
A. Donald Trump
B. Chet Simmons
C. Burt Reynolds
D. Paul Tagliabue
Answer on page 96.

15. Who has the record for most career passing yards in USFL history?
A. Jim Kelly
B. Steve Young
C. Bobby Hebert
D. Greg Landry
Answer on page 96.

EQUIPMENT MANAGERS

1. What piece of equipment were NFL players required to wear in games for the first time in 1943?
A. Shoulder pads
B. Helmets
C. Cleats
D. Protective Cups
Answer on page 96.

2. Who was the NFL's first regular quarterback to wear glasses?
A. Bob Griese
B. Brian Griese
C. Jim McMahon
D. Don Strock
Answer on page 96.

3. Who was the first NFL player to wear a shield on his facemask?
A. Jim McMahon
B. LaDainian Tomlinson
C. Mark Mullaney
D. Jared Allen
Answer on page 96.

4. This quarterback was the last position player to use the single-bar facemask.
A. Jeff Hostetler
B. Phil Simms
C. Randall Cunningham
D. Joe Theismann
Answer on page 97.

5. This player was the first to wear what came to be known as a facemask.
A. Bronko Nagurski
B. Jim Brown
C. Otto Graham
D. Johnny Unitas
Answer on page 97.

GAME-CHANGERS

Through the years, a handful of players have been able to find loopholes in hopes of gaining an extra edge over the competition. This section lists the name of the player. The challenge is to explain what they did and how their actions ultimately forced a change in the NFL rulebook.

1. Lester Hayes
Answer on page 97.

2. Roy Williams
Answer on page 97.

3. Jimmy Graham
Answer on page 97.

4. Emmitt Smith
Answer on page 97.

5. Hines Ward
Answer on page 97.

6. Greg Pruitt
Answer on page 98.

7. Ricky Williams
Answer on page 98.

8. Tom Dempsey
Answer on page 98.

9. Ken Stabler
Answer on page 98.

10. Bronko Nagurski
Answer on page 99.

PLAYERS

ANSWERS

1. D—Thomas had seven sacks in a November 1990 game against the Seahawks.

2. D—Strahan had 22.5 sacks in 2001.

3. D—Jones had sacks in 11 straight games, from October 18, 2018, to December 23, 2018.

4. C—Carr was sacked a whopping 76 times in 2002 with the Texans.

5. A—Jones used to use the head slap to gain an edge on the offensive lineman.

6. D—Favre was sacked 525 times over the course of his career.

7. D—Sanders was an excellent punt returner, but only took three kickoffs back for touchdowns in his career.

8. Julian Edelman. The former college quarterback, who transitioned to receiver and returner when he reached the NFL, also saw some reps at defensive back in 2011.

9. LaDainian Tomlinson had 31 touchdowns and 186 points with San Diego in 2006.

10. A—Rice has 208 career touchdowns.

11. Drew Bledsoe attempted 70 passes in a 1994 overtime win against the Vikings without a pick, giving him the league record.

12. B—Andersen played in 382 career regular-season games.

13. D—Marshall started 270 consecutive regular-season games.

14. C—Brady started every game from September 2001 to September 2008, and from October 2016 until the present (through 2018 season).

15. A—Feagles amassed 71,211 punting yards over the course of his career with the Patriots, Eagles, Cardinals, Seahawks, and Giants. For what it's worth, Feagles also holds the NFL record for most punts in a career with 1,713.

16. Chris Gardocki, who had 1,177 straight punts without a block. He punted for the Bears, Colts, Browns, and Steelers over the course of his career.

17. All three played quarterback and punted, a unique skillset that managed to keep the opposition on its toes.

18. George Blanda. The quarterback/kicker played 26 seasons in professional football.

19. D—Milburn turned the trick in a 1995 game against the Seahawks when he singlehandedly accounted for 404 total yards, including 101 yards rushing and 133 yards on kick returns.

20. A—Smith finished his career with 21,579 yards from scrimmage, second only to Rice's 23,540.

21. D—Sligh, a defensive tackle who played one season with the Raiders in 1967, was 7-feet.

22. B—Shapiro was 5-foot-1. He played one game for the Staten Island Stapletons of the NFL in 1929.

23. D—Okoye had an amazing journey to the National Football League. When he was 12, he moved from Nigeria to Alabama and tested into the ninth grade. He graduated from high school at 16 and went to Louisville, eventually leaving after three years and joining the NFL at the age of 19. He was taken in the first round of the 2007 draft by the Texans, and played his first professional game at 20 years and 91 days.

24. B—Blanda appeared in the final game of his career—as a kicker with the Raiders in the 1975 postseason—at 48 years and 109 days.

25. 1-B, 2-C, 3-A, 4-E, 5-D, 6-I, 7-H, 8-G, 9-F, 10-J

DOUBLE-DIPPING

1. 1-D, 2-A, 3-E, 4-C, 5-B

FANTASTIC FEUDS

1. Take your pick here, but we'll boil it down to most of his quarterbacks. At one point or another, the wide receiver took issue with just about all of his old signal-callers, including Donovan McNabb, Jeff Garcia, and Tony Romo.

2. Randy Moss. Some would argue Revis's feud with Richard Sherman was bigger, but his occasional battles with Moss were memorable affairs. Revis shut down Moss in the two Patriots-Jets games in 2009, while Moss said that offseason he was going to do his best to stay off Revis Island the next year, while Revis called Moss a "slouch" before their first game in 2010.

3. Odell Beckham, Jr. The cornerback has clashed with a variety of different players, but his most notable throwdown came against Beckham when Norman was with the Panthers and OBJ was a member of the Giants. The high point of their feud came in a 2015 game when they tossed out any pretense of competition and straight-up started taking cheap shots at each other on the field.

4. Tom Brady. A rivalry borne out of respect, this one started during a 2012 game when Sherman and the Seahawks beat the Patriots. As Brady walked off the field, Sherman chased after him, asking, "You mad, bro?" Brady got his revenge a few years later when New England beat Seattle in Super Bowl XLIX.

5. Michael Crabtree. The two scrapped in the 2013 NFC title game, with Sherman knocking away a key pass at the end of the game to help secure a Seahawks victory. After the game, Sherman conducted a fiery interview, saying, "I'm the best corner in the game. When you try me with a sorry receiver like Crabtree, that's the result you going to get."

6. Steve Smith. In a 2013 battle between the Patriots and Panthers, Talib and Smith battled throughout the game, but Talib tapped out early because of a hip injury. Meanwhile, the feisty Smith stuck around to lead Carolina to an upset. After the game, Smith told Talib to, "Ice up, son," and later had a t-shirt made with his new slogan.

7. Michael Crabtree. *Again.* The cornerback and receiver have battled multiple times over the years, with Crabtree's chain getting the worst of it. Talib has tried to snatch Crabtree's chain from around his neck, which has set off full-on fights between players. "He has just been wearing that gold chain all year; it's just been growing on me," Talib explained. "I said if he wears that chain in front of me, I'm going to snatch it off. He wore it in front of me, so I had to snatch it off."

8. Terrell Suggs. Brady has had his share of rivals over the years, but few have been as consistent as the one he's enjoyed with Suggs, a veteran who got after him when he was with Baltimore. Suggs has said Brady has gotten the benefit of the doubt when it comes to penalty calls, while Brady has mocked Suggs and the Ravens, saying, "They talk a lot for only beating us once in nine years."

9. Conrad Dobler. Bergey, a defensive lineman with the Eagles, and Dobler, an offensive lineman with the Cardinals, Saints, and Bills, had multiple run-ins over the years. In fact, Bergey's career-ending knee injury came on a play in which he was lined up against Dobler. To be fair, Dobler had scraps with several other players over the course of his career, including Mean Joe Greene and Merlin Olsen.

10. Steve Young. Things grew chilly between the two Hall of Fame quarterbacks in Montana's final days with the Niners. Eventually, Montana left San Francisco, and Young took control of the Niners.

CANADIAN CLUBBERS

1. This Heisman Trophy winner actually played for three different CFL teams—the BC Lions, Calgary Stampeders, and Toronto Argonauts. He won back-to-back Grey Cups with Toronto in 1996 and 1997.

2. Moon spent six seasons in the CFL after going undrafted in 1978 out of Washington; he won five Grey Cups in six years with the Edmonton Eskimos before signing with the Oilers in 1984.

3. Wake spent two seasons with the BC Lions and earned the league's Most Outstanding Rookie Award in 2007, as well as the Most Outstanding Defensive Player Award in 2007 and 2008. In all, he recorded 39 sacks over his two seasons in the CFL before signing with the Dolphins.

4. This former Notre Dame star spent two seasons with the Toronto Argonauts. He was a CFL All-Star in 1991, as well as the MVP of the 79th Grey Cup. He would later land in the NFL, playing for the Raiders, Panthers, and Cowboys.

5. Theismann played for the Toronto Argonauts after he couldn't come to terms with the Dolphins. He spent three years in the CFL and was an all-star with the Argos in 1971 and 1973 before jumping to the NFL with the Redskins.

6. The former Cal quarterback played for both the Calgary Stampeders and BC Lions in his eight seasons in the CFL and led Calgary to a Grey Cup in 1964. Kapp ended up as one of the best quarterbacks in the history of the Vikings.

7. The fullback was a star for Hamilton, Saskatchewan, and Toronto, and helped Hamilton win the 1957 Grey Cup. In his six-year CFL career, Gilchrist recorded 4,911 rushing yards, 1,068 receiving yards, and 12 interceptions. He would go on to play for Buffalo and earn a spot on the franchise Wall of Fame.

8. "Swervyn Mervyn" spent six seasons with the BC Lions. He had 399 catches over the course of his CFL career and was named the league's Most Outstanding Player in 1985. He then played for the Raiders in the NFL.

9. The offensive lineman spent five years with Montreal at the start of his career and two with Hamilton at the end of his career. In between, he had stints in the NFL with the Colts and Eagles.

George was a starter on two Grey Cup champions, both coming with the Alouettes.

10. The defensive end spent four years with Calgary at the start of his career and was a Grey Cup champion. A few years later, he was a starter on Denver's team that won Super Bowl XXXIII. He's one of only a handful of players to capture a Grey Cup and Super Bowl title.

CFL—RELATED BONUS QUESTIONS

1. D—Singh, an offensive lineman, was part of a Rams team that won Super Bowl XXXIV and the Los Angeles Xtreme of the XFL—which won the only Million-Dollar Game in league history in 2001. Finally, he was part of a BC Lions team that won the Grey Cup in 2006.

REMEMBERING THE USFL

1. B—Kelly, who threw 83 touchdown passes in two seasons for the Houston Gamblers, tossed for 574 yards in a 1985 game.

2. New Jersey's Herschel Walker ran for 233 yards against Houston on April 7, 1985.

3. Michigan and Los Angeles played, and the Los Angeles Express won, 27–21.

4. C—The Breakers moved from Boston to New Orleans to Portland.

5. The Breakers and the Washington Federals.

6. Walker, Flutie, Mike Rozier, and Archie Griffin.

7. A—The Stars went 48-13-1 (including the playoffs) and took home two of the three USFL championships.

8. B—Young played with Los Angeles before going on to the NFL.

9. B—Philadelphia's Bryant was named league MVP in 1983.

10. A—Marino was taken first in 1983 by Los Angeles, but ended up going to the NFL to play for Miami instead.

11. A—The Stallions took Rice with the first overall pick in the 1985 draft. He ended up opting for San Francisco and the NFL.

12. D—Mora won 48 games (including the postseason) while coaching Philadelphia/Baltimore for three seasons.

13. 1-D; 2-A; 3-B; 4-E; 5-C.

14. B—Simmons was the first commissioner, and held the job from 1982–85.

15. C—Hebert threw for 10,039 yards in USFL action, good for the league mark.

EQUIPMENT MANAGERS

1. B—Helmets. Remarkably, players were not required to wear helmets until 1943; prior to that year, many had their head covered with some form of leather strap. Before the invention of the helmet, players would often grow their hair long, because they believed it would protect their heads.

2. A—Bob Griese. The league's first bespectacled quarterback tried contacts for a stretch when he had vision troubles, but made the move to glasses in 1977.

3. C—Mullaney, a former defensive end with the Vikings, is believed to be the first player to wear a protective shield over his facemask—he started in 1984 to protect a healing eye injury.

These days, tinted visors are outlawed, unless a player gets special dispensation from his doctor. Clear shields are allowed for anyone.

4. D—Theismann was the last non-punter or kicker to use the single-bar facemask until his retirement in 1985. The last punter to do it was Cleveland's Scott Player in 2007.

5. C—In 1953, Browns founder Paul Brown asked Cleveland equipment manager Leo Murphy to come up with something that would give Graham more protection after the quarterback suffered a cut mouth. Thus, the facemask was born.

GAME-CHANGERS

1. The Raiders defensive back used "Stickum" all over his body in hopes of gaining an extra edge when it came to snagging interceptions. The substance was eventually banned in 1981.

2. The Dallas defensive back inspired the "horse collar" rule after Terrell Owens suffered a broken ankle and Musa Smith a broken leg following tackles by the Dallas defender during which he grabbed the inside collar or the side of the shoulder pads or jersey pads or jersey and pulled the runner toward the ground.

3. The tight end used to dunk the ball over the goalposts after celebrating a touchdown. The move was outlawed at the start of the 2014 season.

4. The record-setting running back used to love to take off his helmet after a touchdown to enjoy the crowd's cheering. The move was outlawed—it's classified as "unsportsmanlike conduct"—in hopes of cutting down on taunting.

5. The former Steelers wide receiver broke the jaw of Cincinnati linebacker Keith Rivers in 2008 with a blindside block.

Subsequently, the league made it illegal to block a defender from the blindside at the head or neck area with the blocker's head/ shoulder or forearm.

6. The running back was one of several players in the 1970s who favored tear-away jerseys as a way to shake off would-be tacklers. He rushed for 1,000 yards in three straight years in the mid-1970s, but the league banned tear-aways in 1979, thanks in no small part to Pruitt's success.

7. It was ruled in 2003 that the dreadlocked running back's hair was an extension of his uniform, and therefore, was OK to use when it came to tackling. It wasn't just offensive players who were at risk here, however, as in 2006, Chiefs running back Larry Johnson dragged Pittsburgh Steelers safety Troy Polamalu down by his hair after an interception. "The dude had hair," Johnson said of his tackle. "What do you want me to do?"

8. The kicker, who was born without toes on his right foot, wore a modified shoe to kick a record-setting 63-yard field goal. The league soon mandated that the kicking surface of a shoe worn by a player with an artificial limb on his kicking foot must conform to that of a normal kicking shoe.

9. In a 1978 game against the Chargers, the Raiders quarterback was trying to lead a last-minute comeback and dropped back to pass from the San Diego 23-yard line. But Stabler was pressured on the play and said after the game he fumbled the ball forward on purpose. The ball rolled forward, and Oakland players Pete Banaszak and Dave Casper shoveled the ball into the end zone, where Casper fell on it for what turned out to be the game-winning score. During the offseason, the league added a provision to the rule book about fumbles after the two-minute warning that allows only the player who fumbled the ball to advance it.

10. The legendary Nagurski was the inspiration for a rule after a controversial finish to the 1932 NFL title game between the Bears and Portsmouth Spartans. At the time, a forward pass was only legal if it was thrown from at least five yards behind the line of scrimmage, and Nagurski delivered a key pass late in the contest after only a couple of steps off the line of scrimmage. However, the Portsmouth coach argued Nagurski wasn't five yards behind the line of scrimmage when he threw the pass. Ultimately, the call stood, and the Bears went on to win 9–0. The following season, the league declared that forward passes could be made from anywhere behind the line of scrimmage.

COACHES

QUESTIONS

"Gentlemen, we will chase perfection, and we will chase it relentlessly, knowing all the while we can never attain it. But along the way, we shall catch excellence."
—*Vince Lombardi*

Coaching in the NFL these days can be a savage, unforgiving business. If you're not a winner by your third season, you're on the hot seat, and will be out the door in a blink. That's if everything goes well—some owners will start to get antsy after 16 games. Since 2000, 11 coaches have gone one (year)-and-done when it comes to head coaching stints. (The good news? Some of them get second chances, like Pete Carroll. He was fired after one season with the Jets, but managed to win a Super Bowl with Seattle, his third tour as a head coach.) This chapter honors the men who have become the on-field leaders of their franchises—the decision-makers we call coach.

1. Name the two coaches who have won 100 regular-season games or more, but are winless in the playoffs.
   Answer on page 115.

2. Which NFL coach has the most career wins?
Answer on page 115.

3. Which NFL coach was fastest to 100 wins?
Answer on page 115.

4. Of the coaches with at least 100 games under their belt at the NFL level, how many of them have a career winning percentage of .700 or better?
Answer on page 115.

5. Which NFL coach is the only one in the history of the league with more than 250 wins in fewer than 400 games?
A. Vince Lombardi
B. Chuck Noll
C. Bill Belichick
D. Andy Reid
Answer on page 115.

6. Name the five losingest coaches in NFL history.
Answer on page 115.

7. Six coaches have taken two different teams to the Super Bowl. Name them and the teams they guided to the big game.
Answer on page 115.

8. Three coaches are 0–4 when coaching in the Super Bowl. Name them and the teams they guided to the big game.
Answer on page 115.

9. How many NFL coaches have been a head coach for 50-plus games, but still have a winning percentage of under .300?
Answer on page 116.

10. Where does Vince Lombardi rank on the list of all-time wins for Packers head coaches?
Answer on page 116.

11. Which coach has the most career postseason wins in Green Bay history?
A. Vince Lombardi
B. Mike Holmgren
C. Curly Lambeau
D. Mike McCarthy
Answer on page 116.

12. Who has more wins as the head coach of the Giants?
A. Ray Perkins
B. Dan Reeves
C. Tom Coughlin
D. Bill Parcells
Answer on page 116.

13. Who are the three coaches to win a college national championship and a Super Bowl?
A. Jimmy Johnson, Barry Switzer, and Pete Carroll
B. John Robinson, Bill Belichick, and Howard Schnellenberger
C. George Halas, Tom Landry, and Vince Lombardi
D. Paul Brown, Mike Ditka, and Curly Lambeau
Answer on page 116.

14. Which former NFL head coach also spent time playing professional basketball?
   A. Barry Switzer
   B. Bud Grant
   C. Chuck Fairbanks
   D. Curly Lambeau
   Answer on page 116.

15. Tom Landry became a legendary head coach with the Cowboys, but as a player, he suited up for one of Dallas's NFC East rivals. Which team was it?
   A. Washington
   B. New York Giants
   C. Philadelphia
   Answer on page 116.

16. Which former Redskins coach won the national racquetball title in the 35-and-over division?
   A. Joe Gibbs
   B. Richie Petitbon
   C. Steve Spurrier
   D. Jack Pardee
   Answer on page 116.

17. True or False: Jack Del Rio is the only head coach of the Raiders since 1998 to have a winning percentage of .500 or better.
   Answer on page 116.

18. This coach is credited with several inventions, including hiring full-time assistants, the facemask, the creation of the practice squad, and the draw play.
   A. Vince Lombardi

B. Paul Brown
C. George Halas
D. Curly Lambeau
Answer on page 116.

19. Who was the youngest head coach in NFL history?
  A. Sean McVay
  B. Pappy Lewis
  C. Mike Vrabel
  D. Lane Kiffin
  Answer on page 116.

20. This coach's team holds the mark for most consecutive wins (regular season and postseason combined).
  A. Vince Lombardi
  B. Mike Holmgren
  C. Bill Belichick
  D. Paul Brown
  Answer on page 116.

21. The Steelers have set the standard when it comes to stability at the head coaching position—they have had just three coaches since 1969. Name them, and how many Super Bowls they have won.
  Answer on page 117.

22. This rule, enacted in 2003, mandates that teams interview minority candidates for head coaching jobs. It has led to the inclusion of more minorities in coaching and administrative positions around the league.
  Answer on page 117.

23. This coach is credited with initially using the term "sack" to describe tackling a quarterback behind the line of scrimmage.
A. George Halas
B. George Allen
C. Mike Ditka
D. Vince Lombardi
Answer on page 117.

24. This coach had the most years between his first NFL championship and his last.
A. Bill Belichick
B. Tom Landry
C. Vince Lombardi
D. George Halas
Answer on page 117.

25. Who was the oldest coach to win an NFL title?
A. Tom Coughlin
B. Pete Carroll
C. George Halas
D. Dick Vermeil
Answer on page 117.

26. Who was the youngest coach to win a Super Bowl?
A. Jon Gruden
B. Bill Belichick
C. Mike Tomlin
D. Bill Cowher
Answer on page 117.

27. Name the coach with an NFL-best six championships as a head coach, since 1933.
Answer on page 117.

28. Which coach holds the record for most consecutive division championships?
A. Tom Landry
B. Bud Grant
C. Chuck Noll
D. Bill Belichick
Answer on page 117.

29. Which coach holds the record for most regular-season wins with one team?
A. Chuck Noll
B. Bill Walsh
C. George Halas
D. Don Shula
Answer on page 117.

30. Who was the only coach to win three Super Bowls with three different quarterbacks?
A. Vince Lombardi
B. Joe Gibbs
C. Chuck Noll
D. Tom Landry
Answer on page 118.

FAMOUS FEUDS

Coaches consider themselves part of a fraternity—a unique brotherhood, bound by the high-stress nature of life in the National Football League. But like any group of brothers, not everyone gets along all the time. We'll give you the name of a coach, and you tell us his *coaching* rival and something about the nature of their rivalry.

1. Mike Ditka
   Answer on page 118.

2. Kevin Gilbride
   Answer on page 118.

3. Jimmy Johnson
   Answer on page 118.

4. Bill Belichick
   Answer on page 118.

5. Jim Harbaugh
   Answer on page 118.

6. George Allen
   Answer on page 119.

7. Josh McDaniels
   Answer on page 119.

8. Forrest Gregg
   Answer on page 119.

9. Bill Walsh
   Answer on page 119.

10. Mike Shanahan
    Answer on page 119.

COACHING TREES

"When you're an assistant and you've been on a few staffs, you're on all kinds of trees. It's a forest."
—*Former 49ers and Lions head coach Steve Mariucci.*

Coaches all come from somewhere, and many of them can trace their professional lineage back to their work as an assistant under a mentor. In this section, the mentor is provided. Name at least five coaches to come from that "tree" who have gone on to become head coaches in the NFL.

1. Bill Belichick
   Answer on page 120.

2. Andy Reid
   Answer on page 120.

3. Mike Holmgren
   Answer on page 120.

4. Bill Parcells
   Answer on page 120.

5. Bill Walsh
   Answer on page 120.

COACHING CAROUSEL
Which coach holds the record for most wins for each franchise?

AFC EAST

1. Buffalo
   Answer on page 120.

2. Miami
   Answer on page 120.

3. New England
   Answer on page 120.

4. New York Jets
   Answer on page 120.

AFC NORTH

1. Baltimore
   Answer on page 120.

2. Cincinnati
   Answer on page 121.

3. Cleveland
   Answer on page 121.

4. Pittsburgh
   Answer on page 121.

AFC SOUTH

1. Houston
   Answer on page 121.

2. Indianapolis
   Answer on page 121.

3. Jacksonville
   Answer on page 121.

4. Tennessee
   Answer on page 121.

AFC WEST

1. Denver
   Answer on page 121.

2. Kansas City
   Answer on page 121.

3. Los Angeles Chargers
   Answer on page 121.

4. Oakland
   Answer on page 121.

NFC EAST

1. Dallas
   Answer on page 121.

2. Philadelphia
   Answer on page 121.

3. New York Giants
   Answer on page 121.

4. Washington
   Answer on page 121.

NFC NORTH

1. Chicago
   Answer on page 121.

2. Detroit
   Answer on page 122.

3. Green Bay
   Answer on page 122.

4. Minnesota
   Answer on page 122.

NFC SOUTH

1. Atlanta
   Answer on page 122.

2. Carolina
   Answer on page 122.

3. New Orleans
   Answer on page 122.

4. Tampa Bay
   Answer on page 122.

NFC WEST

1. Arizona
   Answer on page 122.

2. Los Angeles Rams
   Answer on page 122.

3. San Francisco
   Answer on page 122.

4. Seattle
   Answer on page 122.

FIRST DOWN

1. Match these men with their *initial* stop as head coach in the National Football League:

1. Pete Carroll	A. Baltimore Colts
2. Bill Belichick	B. Philadelphia Eagles
3. Bill Parcells	C. Denver Broncos
4. Don Shula	D. Indianapolis Colts
5. Tony Dungy	E. Los Angeles Raiders
6. Andy Reid	F. Houston Oilers
7. Josh McDaniels	G. New York Giants
8. Bruce Arians	H. New England Patriots
9. Don Coryell	I. New York Jets
10. Chuck Fairbanks	J. Tampa Bay Bucs
11. Mike Shanahan	K. Cleveland Browns
12. Dom Capers	L. St. Louis Cardinals
13. Tony Sparano	M. Los Angeles Rams
14. Chuck Knox	N. Miami Dolphins
15. Jeff Fisher	O. Carolina Panthers

   Answer on page 122.

LAST CALL

1. Match these men with their *final* stop as head coach in the National Football League:

1. Bill Parcells	A. LA Rams
2. Vince Lombardi	B. New Orleans
3. Paul Brown	C. Kansas City
4. Marty Schottenheimer	D. Miami
5. Chuck Knox	E. Atlanta
6. Mike Holmgren	F. Cincinnati
7. Dick Vermeil	G. Arizona
8. Jimmy Johnson	H. San Diego
9. Jerry Glanville	I. Dallas
10. George Seifert	J. Washington
11. Buddy Ryan	K. Detroit
12. Rich Kotite	L. Carolina
13. Bobby Ross	M. Baltimore
14. Ted Marchibroda	N. Seattle
15. Hank Stram	O. New York Jets

Answer on page 122.

COACHES

ANSWERS

1. Jim Mora, Marvin Lewis

2. Don Shula with 328

3. George Halas did it before the start of his 13th season as head coach of the Bears.

4. Three—John Madden at .759, Vince Lombardi at .738, and George Allen at .712.

5. C—Bill Belichick

6. Dan Reeves and Jeff Fisher are tied with 165 career losses, while Tom Landry is third with 162 career defeats. Don Shula is fourth with 156 losses, and Tom Coughlin is fifth with 150 career losses.

7. John Fox—Denver and Carolina; Don Shula—Baltimore and Miami; Bill Parcells—New York Giants and New England; Dan Reeves—Denver and Atlanta; Dick Vermeil—Philadelphia and St. Louis; Mike Holmgren—Green Bay and Seattle.

8. Bud Grant was 0–4 with the Vikings in the Super Bowl. Dan Reeves was 0–3 with the Broncos and 0–1 with the Falcons. And Marv Levy was 0–4 with the Bills in Super Bowl action.

9. 7—Bert Bell, Hue Jackson, Steve Spagnuolo, Gus Bradley, David Shula, Jimmy Phelan, Dave McGinniss.

10. Third, trailing Curly Lambeau with 209 and Mike McCarthy with 125. Lombardi had 89.

11. D—McCarthy, with 10 playoff wins.

12. C—Coughlin is second all-time in franchise history with 102 wins. Steve Owen, who coached the team from 1930 to 1953, is first with 153.

13. A—Johnson, Switzer, and Carroll

14. B—After playing college basketball at the University of Minnesota, Grant averaged 2.6 points per game in two seasons with the Minneapolis Lakers.

15. B—Landry was a defensive back and punter for five seasons with the Giants and one for the Yankees.

16. A—Gibbs won the national 35-and-over U.S. Racquetball Championship in 1976.

17. False—Del Rio was 25–23 in his two-plus years as head coach of the Raiders, while Jon Gruden was 42–38 in his years helming the Raiders and Hue Jackson was 8–8.

18. B—Brown, who coached the Bengals and Browns, was the father of many aspects of the modern game that are still in use today.

19. B—Art "Pappy" Lewis was 27 when he was named head coach of the Cleveland Rams in 1938.

20. C—Belichick and the Patriots won 21 consecutive games between 2003 and 2004, setting the NFL record.

21. Chuck Noll won four as the coach from 1969 to 1991. Bill Cowher won one in his tenure, which stretched from 1992 until 2006. And Mike Tomlin has also won one Super Bowl in his time at the head of the Steelers—from 2007 to 2018.

22. The Rooney Rule, named after Dan Rooney, the former owner of the Steelers.

23. B—According to a story told by Marv Levy to the Rochester *Democrat & Chronicle*, it was Allen. Levy was an assistant to Allen, and he heard Allen use it as a pun during a motivational speech. "George was talking the night before in the team meeting about playing the Dallas Cowboys and their quarterback, Craig Morton. The term had never been used. It was always, 'Tackle the QB for a loss.' But the night before the game, George goes, 'Before we play those Dallas Cowboys, we're going to take that Morton salt and pour him into a sack.' That was the inspiration for it."

24. D—Halas. He won championships with the Bears in both 1921 and 1963, a stretch of 42 years.

25. C—Halas. He was 68 when he won his final title in 1963.

26. C—Tomlin was 36 when his Steelers beat the Cardinals in Super Bowl LIII.

27. Bill Belichick is the only NFL coach with six championships since the league began postseason play in 1933. (If you count the AAFC, Paul Brown had seven.)

28. D—As of the end of the 2018 season, Belichick's consecutive run of division titles is at 10 straight.

29. C—Halas has 318 career regular-season victories as head coach of the Bears. He had 19 of them for the Decatur Staleys and Chicago Staleys, who later became the Bears.

30. B—Gibbs won three Super Bowls with three different starting quarterbacks when he was with the Redskins—Joe Theismann, Doug Williams, and Mark Rypien.

FAMOUS FEUDS

1. Buddy Ryan. Ryan and Ditka worked together in Chicago when Ryan served as the Bears' defensive coordinator, and the two always maintained a tenuous relationship in Chicago. But after Ryan left to become head coach of the Eagles, the gloves came off, and the two spent the next few seasons sniping at each other.

2. Buddy Ryan. Another coach who didn't get along with the feisty Ryan, as the two once came to blows on the sideline while serving as assistant coaches with the Oilers.

3. Buddy Ryan. When the two were coaching against each other in the NFC East in the 1990s, there was certainly no love lost, especially after Johnson accused Ryan's Eagles of targeting his kicker.

4. Eric Mangini. The Patriots coach has rankled many across the league with his success over multiple decades, but his former defensive coordinator likely got under his skin when he took the Jets head coaching job in 2006.

5. Pete Carroll. Harbaugh, the former coach of the Niners, rubbed Carroll the wrong way in the halcyon days of the Seattle-San Francisco rivalry. But it was a feud that had its roots in college when Harbaugh was the head coach at Stanford and Carroll was at USC and Harbaugh was perceived to have run up the score on the Trojans in a 2009 game. During the postgame handshake, Carroll could be heard exclaiming "What's your deal?" to Harbaugh, and a rivalry was born.

6. Tom Landry. This one proves the NFC East battles have always been spicy. Allen's Redskins and Landry's Cowboys embraced the hate in the 1970s. The fiery, passionate Allen was a terrific counterpoint to the cool and reserved Landry.

7. Todd Haley. The two were AFC rivals in November 2010 when McDaniels's Broncos crushed Haley and the Chiefs, 49–29. After the game when the two went in for the traditional postgame handshake, Haley refused, pointed a finger at McDaniels, and said, "There's a lot of [expletive] being talked about you." Haley would later apologize for the incident.

8. Mike Ditka. The Bears and Packers have always been rivals, but a 1986 game set the stage for a feud between the coaches. At the end of a play, Green Bay's Charles Martin picked up Chicago quarterback Jim McMahon and drove his shoulder into the turf, leading to an injury, and—in all likelihood—a chance for the Bears to repeat as champions. The two coaches were at odds for the rest of their careers.

9. Mike Ditka. This rivalry was weight-based. The two coaches clashed in 1984 when Walsh unveiled his "Angus" backfield near the goal line against Chicago, featuring 260-pound guard Guy McIntyre as a blocking back. San Francisco won, 23–0, and after the game, the 49ers taunted the Bears, telling them to "bring your offense" next time. The following year, Chicago beat San Francisco, 26–10, and Ditka unveiled his "Refrigerator" backfield, letting 310-pound William Perry run the ball as the Bears ran out the clock.

10. Dan Reeves. While Shanahan had his share of feuds with others, his greatest coaching rivalry was with Reeves, who was head coach of the Broncos when he was the offensive coordinator. Shanahan and quarterback John Elway were accused of conspiring to remove Reeves from the job. While Elway and Shanahan deny wrongdoing, regardless, the clear enmity that still exists between them makes it one of the NFL's more intriguing coaching feuds.

COACHING TREES

1. Charlie Weis, Romeo Crennel, Bill O'Brien, Eric Mangini, Mike Vrabel, Matt Patricia, and Brian Flores.

2. Brad Childress, Ron Rivera, Sean McDermott, John Harbaugh, Matt Nagy, Steve Spagnuolo, Leslie Frazier, Pat Shurmur, Todd Bowles, and Doug Pederson.

3. Jon Gruden, Andy Reid, Steve Mariucci, Ray Rhodes, Jon Gruden, Dick Jauron, and Mike Sherman.

4. Bill Belichick, Sean Payton, Mike Zimmer, Freddie Kitchens, Tom Coughlin, Romeo Crennel, and Al Groh.

5. Mike Holmgren, Jim Fassel, Paul Hackett, Sam Wyche, George Seifert, and Dennis Green.

COACHING CAROUSEL

AFC East

1. Marv Levy, 112–70–0

2. Don Shula, 257–133–2

3. Bill Belichick, 225–79–0

4. Weeb Ewbank, 71–77–6

AFC North

1. John Harbaugh, 104–72–0

2. Marvin Lewis, 131–122–3

3. Paul Brown, 158–48–8

4. Chuck Noll, 193–148–1

AFC South

1. Gary Kubiak, 61–64–0

2. Tony Dungy, 85–27–0

3. Tom Coughlin, 68–60–0

4. Jeff Fisher, 142–120–0

AFC West

1. Mike Shanahan, 138–86–0

2. Hank Stram, 124–76–10

3. Sid Gillman, 86–53–6

4. John Madden, 103–32–7

NFC East

1. Tom Landry, 250–162–6

2. Andy Reid, 130–93–1

3. Steve Owen, 153–100–17

4. Joe Gibbs, 154–94–0

NFC North

1. George Halas, 318–148–31

2. Wayne Fontes, 66–67–0

3. Curly Lambeau, 209–104–21

4. Bud Grant, 158–96–5

NFC South

1. Mike Smith, 66–46–0

2. John Fox, 73–71–0

3. Sean Payton, 118–74–0

4. Jon Gruden, 57–55–0

NFC West

1. Bruce Arians, 49–30–1

2. John Robinson, 75–68–0

3. George Seifert, 98–30–0

4. Pete Carroll, 89–54–1

FIRST DOWN

1. 1-I, 2-K, 3-G, 4-A, 5-J, 6-B, 7-C, 8-D, 9-L, 10-H, 11-E, 12-O, 13-N, 14-M, 15-F.

LAST CALL

1. 1-I, 2-J, 3-F, 4-H, 5-A, 6-N, 7-C, 8-D, 9-E, 10-L, 11-G, 12-O, 13-K, 14-M, 15-B.

THE LIGHTER SIDE

QUESTIONS

With the talk of protecting the shield, uniform regulations that are specific down to the length of the towel that's allowed to be displayed outside your pants, and the dress code for coaches, the world of professional football is usually a pretty buttoned-up environment. But over the years, there have been plenty who have flown an individualistic flag. From Duane Thomas to Hollywood Henderson to Terrell Owens to Chad Johnson to Martellus Bennett, plenty of guys have been known to have some fun when it comes to speaking with the media, as well as doing their part to keep things loose on the field. This chapter celebrates the characters of the game, as well as some more of the NFL's occasional offbeat history.

NICKNAME NONSENSE
Match the player with his nickname:

1.	O. J. Simpson	A.	Night Train
2.	Deion Sanders	B.	Concrete Charlie
3.	Marshawn Lynch	C.	Megatron
4.	Michael Irvin	D.	Sweetness
5.	Stephen Baker	E.	The Ghost
6.	Dick Lane	F.	He Hate Me

7. Chuck Bednarik   G. Juice
8. Calvin Johnson   H. Prime Time
9. Christian Okoye   I. Deacon
10. Walter Payton   J. White Shoes
11. David Jones   K. Beast Mode
12. Elroy Hirsch   L. The Minister of Defense
13. Dave Casper   M. The Touchdown Maker
14. Billy Johnson   N. The Refrigerator
15. Rod Smart   O. Big Game
16. Andre Rison   P. Captain Comeback
17. Reggie White   Q. Nigerian Nightmare
18. Kenny Stabler   R. Crazylegs
19. Joe Namath   S. The Snake
20. William Perry   T. Mercury
21. Eugene Morris   U. Bambi
22. Torry Holt   V. The Playmaker
23. Jerome Bettis   W. Broadway Joe
24. Roger Staubach   X. Bad Moon
25. Lance Alworth   Y. The Bus

Answer on page 143.

WHO SAID IT? OUR FAVORITE QUOTES

1. "I'm kind of like a black unicorn out there. It's amazing to watch. You go out there and you see a big, black guy running down the field, it's usually me."
    A. Duane Thomas
    B. Martellus Bennett
    C. Najeh Davenport
    D. Bruce Smith
    Answer on page 143.

2. Prior to Super Bowl XVIII, Washington's Joe Jacoby said he'd run over his mother if it meant getting his hands on the title. One of the Raiders said, "I'd run over Joe's Mom too." Who said it?
A. Lyle Alzado
B. Marcus Allen
C. Jack Squirek
D. Matt Millen
Answer on page 143.

3. "Nobody in football should be called a genius. A genius is a guy like Norman Einstein."
A. Ray Lewis
B. John Riggins
C. Joe Theismann
D. Mike Ditka
Answer on page 143.

4. On Terry Bradshaw: "He couldn't spell 'cat' if you spotted him the 'C' and the 'T'."
A. Howie Long
B. Hollywood Henderson
C. Jimmy Johnson
D. Michael Strahan
Answer on page 143.

5. "I may be dumb, but I'm not stupid."
A. Terry Bradshaw
B. Brett Favre
C. Hollywood Henderson
D. Deion Sanders
Answer on page 143.

6. "We can't run. We can't pass. We can't stop the run. We can't stop the pass. We can't kick. Other than that, we're just not a very good football team right now."
A. Bruce Coslet
B. Sam Wyche
C. Jim Mora
D. Mike Ditka
Answer on page 143.

7. On how you pay a fine: "When you're rich, you don't write checks. Straight cash, homey."
A. Warren Sapp
B. Christian Fauria
C. Randy Moss
D. Jim McMahon
Answer on page 143.

8. "I'm just here so I won't get fined."
A. Randy Moss
B. Ray Lewis
C. Marvin Harrison
D. Marshawn Lynch
Answer on page 144.

9. When asked about the challenge of trying to develop chemistry with two different quarterbacks, this player shrugged and said: "I've dated two girls at the same time before."
A. Terrell Owens
B. Martellus Bennett
C. Jerry Rice
D. Marshawn Lynch
Answer on page 144.

10. "Sure, luck means a lot in football. Not having a good quarterback is bad luck."
A. Don Shula
B. Vince Lombardi
C. George Halas
D. Paul Brown
Answer on page 144.

11. "If I drop dead tomorrow, at least I'll know I died in good health."
A. Mike Ditka
B. Bum Phillips
C. Jim Mora
D. Bill Belichick
Answer on page 144.

12. "Most football players are temperamental. That's 90 percent temper and 10 percent mental."
A. William "The Refrigerator" Perry
B. Jim McMahon
C. Doug Plank
D. Richard Dent
Answer on page 144.

13. "I don't know. It isn't like I came down from Mount Sinai with the tabloids."
A. Ron Meyer
B. John McKay
C. Hank Stram
D. Bum Phillips
Answer on page 144.

14. "I don't think anyone on this team knows what 'schism' is, let alone could use it in a sentence. I thought it was an STD when I first heard it and was like 'Whoa, we preach abstinence in these parts.'"
A. Jim McMahon
B. Michael Bennett
C. Martellus Bennett
D. Jared Allen
Answer on page 144.

15. "I feel like I'm the best, but you're not going to get me to say that."
A. Terrell Owens
B. Deion Sanders
C. Jerry Rice
D. Randy Moss
Answer on page 144.

16. One NFL coach on his team's execution: "I think it's a good idea."
A. John McKay
B. Steve Spurrier
C. Mike Ditka
D. Bill Belichick
Answer on page 144.

17. "I love me some me!"
A. Ray Lewis
B. Terrell Owens
C. Shannon Sharpe
D. Conrad Dobler
Answer on page 144.

18. "If you're mad at your kid, you can either raise him to be a nose tackle or send him out to play on the freeway. It's about the same."
A. Bob Golic
B. Warren Sapp
C. Vince Wilfork
D. Fred Smerlas
Answer on page 144.

19. "My knees look like they lost a knife fight with a midget."
A. Mean Joe Greene
B. Jason Taylor
C. E. J. Holub
D. Too Tall Jones
Answer on page 144.

20. "I wouldn't ever set out to hurt anyone deliberately unless it was important. Like a league game."
A. Conrad Dobler
B. Jack Tatum
C. Dick Butkus
D. Bubba Smith
Answer on page 144.

21. Which one of his quarterbacks was Mike Ditka talking about when he said of his signal-caller, post-shoulder surgery: "The shoulder surgery was a success (but) the lobotomy failed"?
Answer on page 144.

22. "I've been big ever since I was little."
A. William Perry
B. Ted Washington
C. Art Donovan
D. Deacon Jones
Answer on page 145.

23. "You play to win the game. Hello?"
A. Herm Edwards
B. Dennis Green
C. Bill Parcells
D. Dan Reeves
Answer on page 145.

24. "Playoffs? Playoffs? Don't talk about playoffs! You kidding me? Playoffs? I just hope we can win another game!"
A. Mike Ditka
B. Jim Mora, Sr.
C. Jim Mora, Jr.
D. Dennis Green
Answer on page 145.

25. "The Bears are who we thought they were! And we let them off the hook!"
A. Vince Lombardi
B. Don Shula
C. Dennis Green
D. Herm Edwards
Answer on page 145.

CRAZY PLAYS

1. This Miami kicker tried to deliver a pass off a botched field-goal attempt in Super Bowl VII, but had the ball slip badly out his hands. It led to an interception and a Washington touchdown.
   A. Uwe Von Schamann
   B. Garo Yapremian
   C. Pete Gogolak
   D. Adam Vinatieri
   Answer on page 145.

2. Which Vikings defensive end picked up a fumble in a 1964 game against the Niners and ran 66 yards in the wrong direction (he thought it was a touchdown, but it turned out to be a safety)?
   A. Alan Page
   B. Jared Allen
   C. Carl Eller
   D. Jim Marshall
   Answer on page 145.

3. Who was the Giants quarterback who butchered the handoff late in a 1978 game against the Eagles that led to the famed "Miracle at the Meadowlands"?
   A. Phil Simms
   B. Y. A. Tittle
   C. Joe Pisarcik
   D. Jeff Hostetler
   Answer on page 145.

4. Who was the Jets offensive lineman whose backside was the cause of Mark Sanchez's epic "Buttfumble" against the Patriots in 2012?
A. Kevin Mawae
B. Damien Woody
C. D'Brickashaw Ferguson
D. Brandon Moore
Answer on page 145.

5. Name the Dallas defensive lineman who had two separate misplays—one where he tried and failed to recover a blocked field-goal attempt late in a regular-season loss to Miami, and another in a Super Bowl win over Buffalo when he had the ball knocked away on the goal-line after not seeing Don Beebe?
A. Nate Newton
B. Leon Lett
C. Too Tall Jones
D. Harvey Martin
Answer on page 145.

6. Who were the quarterback and wide receiver for the Seahawks when they came up with a touchdown on the infamous "Fail Mary" play in 2012 against the Packers?
Answer on page 145.

7. Name the linebacker who tore his ACL in 2014 after celebrating a sack of Aaron Rodgers with his best imitation of Rodgers's "Discount Double-Check" move.
A. Mike Singletary
B. Stephen Tulloch

C. Von Miller
D. Khalil Mack
Answer on page 145.

8. After a series of laterals, this Miami running back was the one who got the ball over the goal line for the Dolphins on their late score to upset the Patriots at the end of the 2018 season.
A. Kenyan Drake
B. Brandon Bolden
C. Ricky Williams
D. Jay Ajayi
Answer on page 145.

HOME SWEET HOME

1. The Redskins played in which city before moving to Washington?
A. Birmingham
B. Boston
C. Buffalo
D. Bakersfield
Answer on page 146.

2. Which AFC team spent its first three seasons in Dallas as the Texans before moving?
A. Kansas City Chiefs
B. New York Jets
C. Denver Broncos
D. Oakland Raiders
Answer on page 146.

3. Which Illinois city was the original home of the Bears?
   A. Peoria
   B. Joliet
   C. Springfield
   D. Decatur
   Answer on page 146.

4. Which AFC team had to have a "Great Flush" to test the plumbing before they moved into their new home prior to the start of the 1970 season?
   A. New England Patriots
   B. New York Jets
   C. Oakland Raiders
   D. San Diego Chargers
   Answer on page 146.

5. This old stadium was known best for "The Black Hole," home to some of the rowdiest fans in the league.
   A. Oakland Coliseum
   B. Shea Stadium
   C. Municipal Stadium
   D. Three Rivers Stadium
   Answer on page 146.

6. Which team changed its name after seeing an unflattering newspaper headline?
   A. Chicago
   B. San Diego
   C. Houston
   D. New England
   Answer on page 146.

7. Which team had to use a college stadium for home games in 2010 after their home field's roof collapsed?
A. New Orleans
B. Minnesota
C. Detroit
D. Indianapolis
Answer on page 146.

8. Which stadium was measured as the loudest in the league?
A. Arrowhead (Kansas City)
B. Superdome (New Orleans)
C. CenturyLink (Seattle)
D. Soldier Field (Chicago)
Answer on page 146.

9. As of 2018, what is the oldest stadium still in use by the NFL?
A. Soldier Field
B. Lambeau Field
C. Arrowhead Stadium
D. Los Angeles Memorial Coliseum
Answer on page 146.

10. What was the first domed stadium in the NFL?
Answer on page 147.

GOING HOLLYWOOD

1. This former Raider would go on to co-star with John Travolta in "Broken Arrow."
A. Howie Long
B. Bob Golic
C. Marcus Allen
D. Jack Tatum
Answer on page 147.

2. There were several former NFL stars in Adam Sandler's remake of "The Longest Yard." Name them.
Answer on page 147.

3. This Hall of Fame running back played Robert Jefferson in "The Dirty Dozen."
A. O. J. Simpson
B. Jim Brown
C. Walter Payton
D. Franco Harris
Answer on page 147.

4. This ex-defensive tackle who won a Super Bowl would portray a mobster in the Spike Lee movie "The 25th Hour."
A. Tony Siragusa
B. Vince Wilfork
C. Fred Smerlas
D. Warren Sapp
Answer on page 147.

5. True or False: Lawrence Taylor has had many movie roles over the years, but the one he lamented missing out on was as the voice of "Mufasa" in "The Lion King."
Answer on page 147.

6. Which one of these NFL stars was *not* in the movie "Jerry Maguire"?
A. Drew Bledsoe
B. Troy Aikman
C. Warren Moon
D. Raghib Ismail
Answer on page 147.

7. Match the fictional movie quarterback with his team:

1.	Willie Beamen	A.	Los Angeles Rams
2.	Shane Falco	B.	Ohio State
3.	Joe Kingman	C.	Texas State
4.	Joe Pendleton	D.	Washington Sentinels
5.	Paul Crewe	E.	North Dallas Bulls
6.	Stan Gable	F.	Miami Sharks
7.	Joe Kane	G.	Adams College
8.	Seth Maxwell	H.	Boston Rebels
9.	Johnny Utah	I.	ESU
10.	Paul Blake	J.	The Mean Machine

Answer on page 147.

8. Match the former player with the TV show where he was a regular:

1.	Alex Karras	A.	*Hunter*
2.	Merlin Olsen	B.	*Webster*
3.	Fred Dryer	C.	*Brooklyn Nine-Nine*
4.	Ed Marinaro	D.	*Saved By The Bell*
5.	Bob Golic	E.	*Father Murphy*
6.	Dick Butkus	F.	*My Two Dads*
7.	Terry Crews	G.	*Hill Street Blues*

Answer on page 147.

9. Which actor did NOT play a football coach on-screen?
A. John Wayne
B. Gene Hackman
C. Al Pacino
D. Denzel Washington
Answer on page 147.

10. Mark Wahlberg starred in the underdog story of what player who goes from semi-pro, sandlot football to the NFL?
A. Troy Brown
B. Vinny Papale
C. Julian Edelman
D. Steve Gleason
Answer on page 147.

11. Match the player with the date he hosted "Saturday Night Live"
1. Tom Brady
2. Peyton Manning
3. Deion Sanders
4. O. J. Simpson
5. Joe Montana/Walter Payton
6. Frank Tarkenton
7. Alex Karras
8. Carl Weathers

A. Feb. 18, 1995
B. Feb. 2, 1985
C. Jan. 29, 1977
D. April 16, 2005
E. Jan. 30, 1988
F. March 24, 2007
G. Jan. 24, 1987
H. Feb. 25, 1978

Answer on page 147.

12. Match the NFL player or coach with the name of his autobiography:
1. Nate Jackson
2. Ken Stabler
3. Rocky Bleier
4. John Madden
5. Jerry Kramer
6. Walter Payton
7. Art Donovan
8. Dan Pastorini
9. Bo Jackson
10. Julian Edelman

A. *Instant Replay* and *Distant Replay*
B. *Never Die Easy*
C. *Fatso*
D. *Snake*
E. *Slow Getting Up*
F. *Hey, Wait A Minute*
G. *Fighting Back*
H. *Bo Knows Bo*
I. *Taking Flak*
J. *Relentless*

Answer on page 147.

MUSICAL MAYHEM

1. This Hall of Fame defensive back and returner recorded an album that included the single "Must Be The Money."
A. Ty Law
B. Deion Sanders
C. Darrelle Revis
D. Eric Berry
Answer on page 148.

2. This '90s star was frequently seen on the sidelines of Falcons games, and recruited several of them—as well as coach Jerry Glanville—to be in his videos.
A. Ice Cube
B. Hammer
C. Jay-Z
D. Nas
Answer on page 148.

3. Which team recorded "The Super Bowl Shuffle"?
A. Bears
B. Niners
C. Steelers
D. Dolphins
Answer on page 148.

4. Which California team recorded their version of "The Super Bowl Shuffle" at roughly the same time?
A. Chargers
B. Rams
C. Niners
D. Raiders
Answer on page 148.

5. This Steelers quarterback recorded a country album.
A. Ben Roethlisberger
B. Charlie Batch
C. Terry Bradshaw
D. Mark Malone
Answer on page 148.

6. Name the former Dallas quarterback who would go on to record a country album with a group called "Super Boys," which included the song "Oklahoma Nights."
A. Roger Staubach
B. Jason Garrett
C. Quincy Carter
D. Troy Aikman
Answer on page 148.

7. This former Bengal would go on to write several country hits, as well as the song, "I Can't Make You Love Me," which went on to be a smash for Bonnie Raitt.
A. Ickey Woods
B. Mike Krumrie
C. Mike Reid
D. Boomer Esiason
Answer on page 148.

8. This Ravens kicker has impressed listeners in the past with his ability to sing opera.
Answer on page 148.

9. Which two teams had remarkably similar-sounding fight songs?
   A. Houston and Miami
   B. Miami and San Diego
   C. San Diego and Chicago
   D. Chicago and Pittsburgh
   Answer on page 148.

10. This team moved from its original location, but their marching band lived on, and would go on to perform in support of several other NFL teams, including one that eventually moved into their city.
    Answer on page 148.

THE LIGHTER SIDE

ANSWERS

NICKNAME NONSENSE

1. 1-G, 2-H, 3-K, 4-V, 5-M, 6-A, 7-B, 8-C, 9-Q, 10-D, 11-I, 12-R, 13-E, 14-J, 15-F, 16-X, 17-L, 18-S, 19-W, 20-N, 21-T, 22-O; 23-Y; 24-P, 25-U.

WHO SAID IT? OUR FAVORITE QUOTES

1. B—Bennett. He gave himself the nickname, telling reporters in 2012.

2. D—Millen

3. C—Theismann

4. B—Henderson said it when asked about Bradshaw prior to Super Bowl XIII.

5. A—Bradshaw

6. A—Coslet, talking about one of his Cincinnati teams.

7. C—Moss.

8. D—Lynch, explaining why he was at Super Bowl Media Day. He gave the same answer to numerous questions.

9. B—Bennett said it in 2016 with the Patriots, as they were trying to prepare for Tom Brady's Deflategate suspension while also working with Jimmy Garoppolo.

10. A—Shula

11. B—Phillips

12. C—Plank

13. A—Meyer, when he was asked if he felt like he made the right decision starting Jeff George.

14. D—Allen, who was asked to address the possibility of a hostile "schism" growing in the Minnesota locker room between teammates.

15. C—Rice

16. A—McKay, while in the midst of a losing season with the Buccaneers.

17. B—Owens was caught uttering the phrase while on the sidelines as a member of the Niners when San Francisco was facing Atlanta.

18. A—Golic, who played defensive tackle and linebacker in the NFL from 1979 to 1992.

19. C—Holub, a center and linebacker who played professionally from 1961 to 1970, lamenting his many knee surgeries.

20. C—Butkus

21. Jim McMahon

22. A—Perry

23. A—Edwards said it as head coach of the Jets in 2002.

24. B—Mora uttered the infamous line while head coach of the Colts in 2001.

25. C—Green had his famous rant after a 2006 game where his Cardinals suffered a come-from-behind loss to Chicago.

CRAZY PLAYS

1. B—Yapremian's play, known as "Garo's Gaffe," lives on as one of the more memorable plays of an otherwise forgettable game.

2. D—Marshall, who later acquired his nickname "Wrong Way" Marshall for his mistake.

3. C—Pisarcik and Larry Csonka couldn't manage the handoff, which led to a fumble and the late Philly score.

4. D—Moore had been shoved out of his gap by Vince Wilfork, setting up the collision between Sanchez and his offensive lineman.

5. B—Lett's gaffe cost the Cowboys the game against the Dolphins, but Dallas still ended up crushing the Bills in Super Bowl XXVII.

6. Russell Wilson was the quarterback and Golden Tate was the receiver. The touchdown, which sparked the end of the officiating work stoppage, gave Seattle a 14–12 win.

7. B—Tulloch's ill-advised celebration cost him the rest of the season.

8. A—Drake was the guy who snuck past the New England defenders for the touchdown, putting the capper on one of the wildest finishes in recent history.

HOME SWEET HOME

1. B—The Redskins played in Boston from 1932 to 1936 and were known as the Braves, and later, the Redskins.

2. A—The Chiefs spent three seasons in Dallas as the Texans before moving to Kansas City and undergoing a name change.

3. D—Decatur. The Bears played one season—1920—as the Decatur Staleys before moving to Chicago in 1921.

4. A—Patriots. Prior to the second game at Schaefer Stadium, the plumbing was tested at the new venue by having stadium employees simultaneously flush all the toilets in the stadium.

5. A—Oakland. Raiders fans were a wild presence in Oakland, as "The Black Hole" was stocked with all sorts of football-loving crazies.

6. D—The Patriots had initially planned to call themselves "Bay State Patriots," a nod to their Massachusetts roots. But after reportedly seeing a headline that used the phrase "BS Patriots," they thought better of the idea, and changed it instead to "New England" Patriots.

7. B—The Metrodome had an inflatable roof that ended up collapsing in 2010 after a nasty blizzard. The Vikings played one game outdoors at the University of Minnesota and another "home" game in Detroit.

8. A—In Kansas City in 2014, the fans broke the record, checking in at 142.2 decibels, a record that had been held by Seattle.

9. D—The Rams are set to move into a new building in 2020, but for now, they still play in a venue that was built in 1923 and has hosted multiple Olympic ceremonies, as well as USC football and an occasional baseball game.

10. The Houston Astrodome opened to the Oilers in 1968.

GOING HOLLYWOOD

1. A—Long, a Massachusetts native who would star at Villanova and with the Raiders, would also reach the Hall of Fame in 2000.

2. Bill Romanowski, Michael Irvin, Brian Bosworth, and Sean Salisbury.

3. B—Brown, a former NFL MVP, would go on to be a part of several other films, including "He Got Game," "Mars Attacks," and "I'm Gonna Git You Sucka."

4. A—Siragusa played Kostya Novotny in the 2002 film.

5. False. But Taylor has been in several other films, including "The Waterboy," "Shaft," and "Any Given Sunday."

6. D—Ismail was not in the film.

7. 1-F, 2-D, 3-H, 4-A, 5-J, 6-G, 7-I, 8-E, 9-B, 10-C

8. 1-B, 2-E, 3-A, 4-G, 5-D, 6-F, 7-C

9. A—Wayne. Hackman was the coach in "The Replacements," Pacino in "Any Given Sunday" and Washington in "Remember the Titans."

10. B—Wahlberg stars in "Invincible," the story of Papale's journey from down-on-his-luck Philadelphian to special teamer for the Eagles.

11. 1-D, 2-F, 3-A, 4-H, 5-G, 6-C, 7-B, 8-E

12. 1-E, 2-D, 3-G, 4-F, 5-A, 6-B, 7-C, 8-I, 9-H, 10-J

MUSICAL MAYHEM

1. B—Sanders's song was part of the 1994 album entitled "Prime Time."

2. B—Hammer was a friend of the Falcons, and included some of them in his "Too Legit To Quit" video.

3. A—The 1985 Bears recorded the single, which was nominated for a Grammy.

4. B—The Rams recorded "Let's Ram It." It was not nominated for a Grammy.

5. C—Bradshaw's album came out in the mid-1970s. His first single, a cover of Hank Williams' classic "I'm So Lonesome I Could Cry," reached the top 20.

6. D—Aikman teamed with tight end Jay Novacek, special teams coach Joe Avezzano, and former players Randy White and Walt Garrison to form the group.

7. C—Reid and Raitt actually co-wrote that hit, which became a top-10 hit on the adult contemporary charts.

8. Justin Tucker

9. A—The Dolphins' song was first, and the Oilers simply "borrowed" the same melody and just changed the lyrics.

10. The Baltimore Colts Marching Band, which was founded in 1947 and continues to perform today in support of the Ravens.

AWARD-WINNERS

QUESTIONS

Football is the ultimate team game, but that doesn't mean you can't celebrate the work of the individual from time to time. Whether it's the MVP, Rookie of the Year, Coach of the Year, or any other honor you might mention, the NFL takes time at the end of the season to hand out the hardware for some of the best solo performances of the year. Here's the history of some of the most important awards the league has to offer.

The NFL MVP award has gone through a lot of iterations over the years. Known initially as the Gruen Award of Merit (it was sponsored by the Gruen Watch Company), it was then renamed the Joe F. Carr Trophy to honor Carr, the former president of the NFL from 1921 to 1939. The Carr Trophy was awarded by the NFL from 1938 to 1946, the only time the league has officially sanctioned an MVP award. While several outlets have handed out their own MVPs over the years (including *The Sporting News*, the UPI, and the Pro Football Writers Association of the NFL), the de facto honor that is perhaps most recognized today is the one handed out by the Associated Press, which they distributed for the first time in 1957.

The Pro Bowl has also been a longstanding way to celebrate individual success on the field. The game has sort of become a bit of a punchline, but it does have a lengthy history. Pro football's first all-star game took place at the end of the 1939 season at Wrigley Field in Los Angeles. The contest was played again in Los Angeles in 1940, and then in New York and Philadelphia in 1941 and 1942 respectively. In all, the first five contests featured a team of all-stars against that year's league champion. (In the first game, the NFL champion New York Giants beat the All-Stars, 13–10.) It wasn't technically named the "Pro Bowl" until 1950, and the first 21 games were played in Los Angeles. The game then moved over the next seven years before it settled in Hawaii in 1980. There have been various attempts to tinker with the game over the last several years in hopes of making it more competitive—changing the rosters, adding a draft to the mix between league legends, moving the location—but it's still the most derided of the all-star games of the four major sports.

From a broader perspective—and for those who miss out on the MVP—All-Pro honors are perhaps a truer measure of a player's success. Those are handed out to the top two players at their position (a first- and second-team is designated), regardless of whether or not the player is in the AFC or NFC. While the Pro Bowl may have previously been a more estimable honor, these days, it's hard to argue with the idea that an All-Pro berth is more exclusive, and a greater honor than reaching the Pro Bowl. At least twice as many Pro Bowlers are named as compared to the first- and second-team All-Pro slots. In addition, Pro Bowlers often drop out, allowing a lesser player to also receive the honor by default.

With all that being said, let's take a look at some of the NFL's most memorable individual award winners over the years.

MVP MADNESS

1. Who was the first winner of the AP MVP award in 1957?
   A. Otto Graham
   B. Jim Thorpe
   C. Sammy Baugh
   D. Jim Brown
   Answer on page 163.

2. Who is the last non-quarterback to win the AP MVP?
   Answer on page 163.

3. _____ was the last non-offensive player to win AP MVP.
   Answer on page 163.

4. A kicker won an AP MVP award: True or false.
   Answer on page 163.

5. Which of the following positions has never won an AP MVP award?
   A. Defensive tackle
   B. Wide receiver
   C. Quarterback
   D. Running back
   Answer on page 163.

6. Who was the youngest winner of the AP MVP award?
   A. Jim Brown
   B. Adrian Peterson
   C. Dan Marino
   D. Earl Campbell
   Answer on page 163.

7. Who was the oldest winner of the AP MVP award?
  A. Tom Brady
  B. Drew Brees
  C. Brett Favre
  D. Otto Graham
  Answer on page 163.

8. Which team has had the most AP MVP winners in league history?
  A. Packers
  B. Steelers
  C. Redskins
  D. Browns
  Answer on page 164.

9. True or False: Jim Brown is the only four-time winner of the AP MVP.
  Answer on page 164.

10. Match the player with the team he was playing for when he won the AP MVP:

  1. Bert Jones   A. San Francisco 49ers
  2. Norm Van Brocklin   B. Dallas Cowboys
  3. Mark Moseley   C. Denver Broncos
  4. Roman Gabriel   D. Cincinnati Bengals
  5. John Brodie   E. Minnesota Vikings
  6. Alan Page   F. Philadelphia Eagles
  7. Brian Sipe   G. New York Giants
  8. Rich Gannon   H. Baltimore Colts
  9. Emmitt Smith   I. Los Angeles Rams
  10. Shaun Alexander   J. Oakland Raiders
  11. Lawrence Taylor   K. Buffalo Bills

12. Terrell Davis
13. Ken Anderson
14. Terry Bradshaw
15. Thurman Thomas

L. Pittsburgh Steelers
M. Seattle Seahawks
N. Cleveland Browns
O. Washington Redskins

Answer on page 164.

11. Which two of these franchises has *never* had an AP MVP award winner?
A. Green Bay Packers
B. Baltimore Ravens
C. Indianapolis Colts
D. New York Jets
Answer on page 164.

12. Who was the last player to collect an AP MVP and Super Bowl trophy in the same season?
A. Kurt Warner (1999)
B. Terrell Davis (1998)
C. Tom Brady (2007)
D. LaDanian Tomlinson (2006)
Answer on page 164.

13. Which one of these players was *not* a back-to-back MVP winner?
A. Peyton Manning
B. Joe Montana
C. O. J. Simpson
D. Jim Brown
Answer on page 164.

14. Who has won the most AP MVP honors?
A. Jim Brown
B. Steve Young
C. Tom Brady
D. Peyton Manning
Answer on page 164.

15. Which position has won the most AP MVP awards?
A. Running back
B. Quarterback
C. Linebacker
D. Wide receiver
Answer on page 164.

16. What uniform number has produced the most AP NFL MVP award-winners?
Answer on page 164.

17. True or False: There have been two AP MVP winners who have taken home the award playing for different teams.
Answer on page 164.

18. Which two players are tied for the longest span between AP MVP awards?
Answer on page 164.

19. Who was the last player to win the Walter Payton Man of the Year Award and AP MVP in the same season?
A. LaDainian Tomlinson
B. Drew Brees
C. Peyton Manning
D. Aaron Rodgers
Answer on page 164.

20. True or False: No one has ever won the Comeback Player of the Year and AP MVP honors in the same year.
Answer on page 165.

21. How many times have there been co-MVP winners (including winners as voted by the players)? Name the players and the years.
Answer on page 165.

PRO BOWL POSITIVES

1. True or false: Jim Brown was the MVP of the first Pro Bowl.
Answer on page 165.

2. Who has the record for most career points in the Pro Bowl?
A. Morten Andersen
B. Mike Vanderjagt
C. Adam Vinatieri
D. David Akers
Answer on page 165.

3. Who holds the record for most career rushing yards in the Pro Bowl?
A. Walter Payton
B. Adrian Peterson
C. O. J. Simpson
D. Marshall Faulk
Answer on page 165.

4. Legendary Arizona receiver _____ holds the record for most Pro Bowl touchdowns with eight.
Answer on page 165.

5. Who has coached in the most Pro Bowl games in his career?
A. Bill Cowher
B. Andy Reid
C. Bill Belichick
D. Bill Parcells
Answer on page 165.

6. Which coach has the most Pro Bowl wins on his resume?
A. Bill Cowher
B. Andy Reid
C. Bill Belichick
D. Bill Parcells
Answer on page 165.

7. At the 2003 Pro Bowl, an AFC quarterback lamented about his team's "idiot kicker who got liquored up and ran his mouth." Who was it?
A. Tom Brady
B. Peyton Manning
C. Ben Roethlisberger
D. Donovan McNabb
Answer on page 165.

8. Which one of these Pro Bowl passing records does Peyton Manning *not* hold?
A. Touchdown passes, game
B. Touchdown passes, career

C. Passing yards, game
D. Passing yards, career
Answer on page 165.

9. This Jets defensive back got into some hot water when he tackled the Patriots' mascot a few days before one Pro Bowl affair.
A. Antonio Cromartie
B. Darrelle Revis
C. Jamal Adams
D. Calvin Pryor
Answer on page 165.

10. Peyton Manning, Jerry Rice, and Phil Simms were the first three players to win a Super Bowl MVP and a Pro Bowl MVP—not in the same year, but over the course of their careers. Name the fourth.
A. Champ Bailey
B. Randy Moss
C. Ray Lewis
D. Von Miller
Answer on page 165.

11. Of the five players tied with the most career Pro Bowl selections—14—he's the only defensive player among them.
A. Ed Reed
B. Reggie White
C. Merlin Olsen
D. Derrick Brooks
Answer on page 165.

12. This Colts rookie made history in 2018 after being snubbed for the Pro Bowl, but still landing a first-team All-Pro honor. It was the first such discrepancy since the AFL-NFL merger in 1970.
Answer on page 166.

13. Which 2010 Pro Bowl quarterback never started a game in college?
Answer on page 166.

14. Who was the MVP of the highest-scoring Pro Bowl in history?
A. Peyton Manning
B. Marc Bulger
C. Marshall Faulk
D. Chad Ochocinco
Answer on page 166.

15. Who has the most career catches in the Pro Bowl?
A. Larry Fitzgerald
B. Randy Moss
C. Tony Gonzalez
D. Jason Witten
Answer on page 166.

16. Which New York Giants pass catcher set the record for most receptions in one Pro Bowl game?
A. Plaxico Burress
B. Mark Bavaro
C. Victor Cruz
D. Jeremy Shockey
Answer on page 166.

17. Which quarterback has the record for longest completed pass in Pro Bowl history?
A. Peyton Manning
B. Jeff Blake
C. Marc Bulger
D. Tom Brady
Answer on page 166.

18. Who has the record for longest successful run from scrimmage in Pro Bowl history?
A. Marshall Faulk
B. Jim Brown
C. LaDainian Tomlinson
D. O. J. Simpson
Answer on page 166.

19. Which one of these players has *never* won a Pro Bowl MVP award?
A. Mean Joe Greene
B. Randy Moss
C. Kyle Rudolph
D. Nick Foles
Answer on page 166.

20. For three seasons—from 2013 through 2015—the Pro Bowl went with a unique format that had former legends picking teams. Name those legendary "GMs."
Answer on page 166.

ALL-PRO

1. These two players are tied for the most career first-team All-Pro selections with 10.
   A. Jim Brown and Lawrence Taylor
   B. Lawrence Taylor and Anthony Muñoz
   C. Anthony Muñoz and Jerry Rice
   D. Jerry Rice and Jim Otto
   Answer on page 166.

2. Of the 24 players in the history of the National Football League with seven or more All-Pro selections, these two players were the only ones in the history of the NFL to capture All-Pro honors with two or more teams.
   Answer on page 166.

3. Which two quarterbacks are tied for the most All-Pro honors?
   A. Peyton Manning and Otto Graham
   B. Otto Graham and Tom Brady
   C. Tom Brady and Joe Montana
   D. Joe Montana and Dan Marino
   Answer on page 167.

4. Over the course of his career, Peyton Manning threw to how many different first-team All-Pro pass catchers?
   Answer on page 167.

5. Between 2001 and 2018, Tom Brady threw to how many different first-team All-Pro pass catchers?
   Answer on page 167.

6. Among defensive players, these five are tied for the most first-team All-Pro nods with eight: Lawrence Taylor, Joe Schmidt, Reggie White, Bruce Smith and _____ .
Answer on page 167.

7. For the Patriots, between 2001 and 2018, seven players have completed a unique trifecta, all in one year: a first-team All-Pro nod, a Pro Bowl nomination, and a Super Bowl ring, all in one year. Who were they?
Answer on page 167.

8. These two quarterbacks are tied for the top spot among signal-callers when it comes to the most first-team All-Pro nods.
A. Peyton Manning and Otto Graham
B. Otto Graham and Dan Marino
C. Dan Marino and Roger Staubach
D. Roger Staubach and Peyton Manning
Answer on page 167.

9. This pair represents the only two players in NFL history with six or more first-team All-Pro honors who are eligible for the Pro Football Hall of Fame who don't have a spot in Canton.
Answer on page 167.

10. Which one of the following players has *not* been a unanimous first-team All-Pro at some point in his career?
A. Aaron Donald
B. Tom Brady
C. Antonio Brown
D. John Elway
Answer on page 167.

AWARD-WINNERS

ANSWERS

MVP MADNESS

1. D—Brown won the AP award the first two years it was handed out, 1957 and 1958.

2. Adrian Peterson, 2012

3. Lawrence Taylor, 1986

4. True. Mark Moseley, 1982

5. B—A wide receiver has never won an MVP award. For what it's worth, only a handful of positions have been so honored—defensive tackle, quarterback, running back, linebacker, and placekicker are the only five positions that have seen an MVP award.

6. A—Brown won at the age of 21, and a year later at 22. In 2018, Chiefs quarterback Patrick Mahomes tied Walter Payton and Dan Marino as the second-youngest MVPs at the age of 23.

7. A—Brady won the award at the age of 40 following the 2017 season. It was the third time in his career he captured the honor.

8. A—Green Bay players have won the MVP eight times; Brett Favre has won three, Aaron Rodgers has won two, and Jim Taylor, Paul Hornung, and Bart Starr won it once each.

9. False—Brown won it three times, including the first two years the award was given.

10. 1-H, 2-F, 3-O, 4-I, 5-A, 6-E, 7-N, 8-J, 9-B, 10-M, 11-G, 12-C, 13-D, 14-L, 15-K

11. B and D—The Ravens and Jets have never had MVPs.

12. A—Warner won the MVP and led the Rams to the Super Bowl in the same season.

13. C—Simpson won the award in 1973, the only time he was so honored.

14. D—Manning won five.

15. B—Quarterbacks have won the award 43 times.

16. No. 12 has been the most popular number when it comes to AP MVP award winners. Nine players who have worn those digits have won the award that year: Tom Brady (three times), Aaron Rodgers (twice), John Brodie, Ken Stabler, Terry Bradshaw, and Rich Gannon (all once).

17. False. Peyton Manning is the only player in NFL history to win AP MVPs for two different teams—the Broncos and Colts.

18. Jim Brown and Tom Brady both went seven years between MVPs. Brown won his second in 1958 and captured his third in 1965. Meanwhile, Brady won his second in 2010 and his third in 2017.

19. A—In 2006, Tomlinson was a co-winner of the Man of the Year Award with Brees and took home MVP honors the same season as well.

20. True

21. Three times
2003: Peyton Manning and Steve McNair
1997: Barry Sanders and Brett Favre
1960: Norm Van Brocklin and Joe Schmidt

PRO BOWL POSITIVES

1. False—It was Otto Graham. Graham and the American Conference captured a narrow 28–27 win over the National Conference on January 14, 1951, at the Memorial Coliseum in Los Angeles.

2. D—Akers, a six-time Pro Bowler, has 57 career points in the Pro Bowl.

3. A—Payton had 368 rushing yards in his Pro Bowl career.

4. Larry Fitzgerald

5. B—Andy Reid has coached in six Pro Bowls.

6. A—Cowher has led the AFC to four Pro Bowl victories.

7. B—Manning ripped teammate Mike Vanderjagt for his comments about the Colts being unlikely to get any better under then-coach Tony Dungy.

8. A—Marc Bulger of the Rams had four in 2004.

9. C—Adams drew the ire of some New England fans when he delivered a flying hit on Pat Patriot before the 2019 Pro Bowl.

10. D—Miller was named MVP of Super Bowl 50, and a co-MVP of the 2018 Pro Bowl.

11. C—Olsen was voted to the Pro Bowl every year, with the exception of his final season in the NFL.

12. Linebacker Darius Leonard

13. Matt Cassel

14. B—Bulger threw a Pro-Bowl record four touchdown passes to lead the NFC to a comeback 55–52 win over the AFC in February 2004.

15. C—Gonzalez had 49 receptions in the Pro Bowl in his career. For the record, he also holds the mark for the most receiving yards in Pro Bowl action with 746.

16. C—Cruz set the mark with 10 receptions in January 2013. This surpassed the previous mark of nine catches for a record 212 yards (2000 by Randy Moss).

17. B—Blake. The former Bengals quarterback delivered a 93-yard scoring strike to Yancey Thigpen in the 1996 Pro Bowl.

18. A—As a rookie, Faulk had a 49-yard touchdown in 1995. He finished the game with 13 carries for 180 rushing yards.

19. A—Greene was named to 10 Pro Bowls, but never won a Pro Bowl MVP.

20. Michael Irvin, Deion Sanders, Jerry Rice, and Cris Carter.

ALL-PRO

1. D—Otto and Rice have 10 nods each, good enough for best all-time.

2. Peyton Manning and Reggie White. Manning finished as a first-team All-Pro seven years—five nods with the Colts and two with the Broncos. Meanwhile, White was named first-team All-Pro eight times—six with the Eagles and two with the Packers.

3. A—Manning and Graham have each won seven All-Pro awards, the best for any quarterback in the history of the game.

4. In Indianapolis from 1998 through 2011, Marvin Harrison reached All-Pro status three times, while Reggie Wayne, Dallas Clark, and Edgerrin James all did it once. He did not have an All-Pro pass catcher while he was with Denver. In all, that's six.

5. In New England from 2001 through 2018, Rob Gronkowski reached All-Pro status four times, while Wes Welker did it twice and Randy Moss did it once. In all, that's seven.

6. Bill George. The former Bears two-way player made it eight times in his 15-year career.

7. Stephon Gilmore, Ty Law, Richard Seymour, Adam Vinatieri, Rob Gronkowski, Darrelle Revis, and Matthew Slater.

8. A—Manning and Graham are tied with the most first-team All-Pro nods in their careers with seven each.

9. Alan Faneca and Jim Tyrer

10. D—Elway is the only player on the list not to win a unanimous first-team All-Pro spot at some stage of their respective careers. In fact, in an odd quirk, Elway never took home a first-team All-Pro in his playing career. The same was the case for Warren Moon, Roger Staubach, and Troy Aikman.

TEAMS

QUESTIONS

"The beautiful thing about the NFL season is to see a team come together after they get to know each other in the spring and summer. You then go through adversity together and see how you respond. The teams that can respond in a positive way are the teams that are going to be there in the end."
—Aaron Rodgers

"On a team, it's not the strength of the individual players, but it is the strength of the unit and how they all function together."
—Bill Belichick

While we can take time to celebrate individual achievements through the history of the National Football League, it's important to realize that football is the ultimate team game. A celebration of 11, working together, to achieve a common goal. This section celebrates teams and their accomplishments—good or . . . not so good. It also highlights which teams were first in a variety of categories.

1. Which was the only team to pull off the perfect season—
   an undefeated regular season and a Super Bowl title?
   A. The 1985 Bears
   B. The 2007 Patriots
   C. The 1972 Dolphins
   D. The 1989 Niners
   Answer on page 179.

2. Since 1944, only five teams have gone winless over the
   course of a full season. Who were they?
   Answer on page 179.

3. Which two franchises in existence at the dawn of professional football in 1920 are still active today?
   Answer on page 179.

4. Which NFL franchise has moved the most?
   A. Raiders
   B. Rams
   C. Cardinals
   D. Chiefs
   Answer on page 179.

5. The latest round of NFL expansion took place in 1995.
   Which two teams were added?
   Answer on page 179.

6. Match the team with its original location/name:
   1. Tennessee Titans   A. Portsmouth
   2. Chicago Bears   B. Chicago/St. Louis/Phoenix
   3. Baltimore Ravens   C. Houston
   4. Indianapolis Colts D. Decatur

5. Washington Redskins   E. Dallas
6. Arizona Cardinals   F. Cleveland
7. Los Angeles Chargers   G. Boston
8. Kansas City Chiefs   H. San Diego
9. Detroit Lions   I. Baltimore

Answer on page 179.

7. Which two teams were involved in the most penalized game in NFL history? (Including penalties that were accepted or declined)
   A. Raiders and Dolphins
   B. Raiders and Cowboys
   C. Raiders and Patriots
   D. Seahawks and Buccaneers
   Answer on page 179–180.

8. Which franchise set the record for most rushing yards in a single season by one team?
   A. The 1978 Patriots
   B. The 1973 Bills
   C. The 1978 Chiefs
   D. The 1972 Dolphins
   Answer on page 180.

9. Which franchise set the record for fewest rushing yards in a single season by one team?
   A. The 1944 Redskins
   B. The 1946 Lions
   C. The 1976 Bucs
   D. The 1940 Eagles
   Answer on page 180.

10. Which franchise set the mark for most net passing yards in a single season?
A. The 2007 Patriots
B. The 2013 Broncos
C. The 2009 Saints
D. The 1978 Chargers
Answer on page 180.

11. Which franchise set the record for fewest net passing yards in a 16-game season by one team?
A. The 1976 Buccaneers
B. The 1982 Patriots
C. The 1991 Colts
D. The 1979 Chiefs
Answer on page 180.

12. Name the two teams who were involved in the highest-scoring regular-season game in NFL history.
Answer on page 180.

13. Match the team with the season record it holds.

1. 2013 Broncos	A.	Most interceptions thrown (48)
2. 1992 Seahawks	B.	Most points at home (329)
3. 2007 Patriots	C.	Fewest points at home (103)
4. 1988 Dolphins	D.	Most field goals (44)
5. 2011 Saints	E.	Fewest interceptions thrown (2)
6. 1977 Buccaneers	F.	Fewest sacks allowed (7)
7. 2011 Niners	G.	Most passes attempted (727)
8. 2012 Lions	H.	Most points (606)
9. 1962 Oilers	I.	Fewest points (140)
10. 2016 Patriots	J.	Most games won, regular season (16)

Answer on page 180.

14. Which team had the longest postseason victory drought?
A. Cardinals
B. Vikings
C. Bears
D. Jets
Answer on page 180.

15. Which eventual Super Bowl champion went five games without scoring a touchdown the year they came away with the title?
A. The 2003 Patriots
B. The 2000 Ravens
C. The 1966 Packers
D. The 1969 Chiefs
Answer on page 180.

NAME GAME
Identify the teams that played in these "Name Games," and why they were so famous.

1. "Ghost to the Post"
Answer on page 180–181.

2. "The Snow Bowl"
Answer on page 181.

3. "The Ice Bowl"
Answer on page 181.

4. "The Fog Bowl"
Answer on page 181.

5. "The Immaculate Reception"
Answer on page 181–182.

6. "Music City Miracle"
Answer on page 182.

7. "The Drive"
Answer on page 182.

8. "The Minneapolis Miracle"
Answer on page 182.

9. "The Greatest Game Ever Played"
Answer on page 182.

10. "4th and 26"
Answer on page 182.

LOGO LOGIC

1. Which team was the first to put a logo on the side of its helmet?
A. Bears
B. Packers
C. Rams
D. Vikings
Answer on page 182–183.

2. Which NFL team has its logo on only one side of its helmet?
A. Panthers
B. Patriots
C. Steelers
D. Raiders
Answer on page 183.

3. Tampa Bay initially had a swashbuckling pirate on the side of its helmets. What was his name?
   A. Captain Morgan
   B. Bucco Bruce
   C. Petey the Pirate
   D. Tampa Tony
   Answer on page 183.

4. _____ current logos are represented with some form of animal.
   Answer on page 183.

5. _____ current logos are represented *primarily* with one letter or a series of initials.
   Answer on page 183.

6. _____ current logos have some sort of human (or human-like) face.
   Answer on page 183.

7. _____ current logos feature some sort of otherwise undefined design as the primary insignia.
   Answer on page 183.

8. Which team had to change its logo because of a potential dispute with the Ford Motor Company?
   A. Jaguars
   B. Panthers
   C. Lions
   D. Broncos
   Answer on page 183.

9. The powder-blue throwbacks for this California-based team are accorded as some of the most popular in the league.
A. Rams
B. Niners
C. Chargers
D. Raiders
Answer on page 183.

10. Which team currently has the longest streak when it comes to helmet design and logo?
A. Packers
B. Eagles
C. Giants
D. Colts
Answer on page 183.

NICKNAME NONSENSE

Match the team with the nickname they were given at some point in franchise history. (Note: This could also refer to the team as a whole, or some of their specific offensive or defensive units):

1. New Orleans	A. Big Blue
2. Chicago	B. Purple People Eaters
3. Dallas	C. Dirty Birds
4. New York Giants	D. Aints
5. Oakland	E. The Electric Company
6. Minnesota	F. Monsters of the Midway
7. Cincinnati	G. America's Team
8. Atlanta	H. Silver and Black
9. Buffalo	I. Gang Green
10. Los Angeles Rams	J. The Hogs
11. New York Jets	K. Orange Crush

12. St. Louis Rams
13. Washington
14. Seattle
15. Denver
16. Jacksonville
17. Pittsburgh

L. Sacksonville
M. The Steel Curtain
N. The Legion of Boom
O. Bungles
P. The Greatest Show on Turf
Q. Fearsome Foursome

Answer on page 184.

ANSWERS

1. C—The 1972 Dolphins were the only team to go wire-to-wire, finishing the season 17–0. The Bears (1985) and Patriots (2007) came the closest, losing one game in each of those years.

2. The 1960 Dallas Cowboys (0–11–1), The 1976 Tampa Bay Buccaneers (0–14), The 1982 Baltimore Colts (0–8–1), The 2008 Detroit Lions (0–16), The 2017 Cleveland Browns (0–16).

3. The Chicago Cardinals (now the Arizona Cardinals) and Decatur Staleys (now the Chicago Bears).

4. B—The Rams have moved three times. Starting in 1946 the Cleveland Rams moved to Los Angeles. In 1995 they relocated to St. Louis and played there until moving back to Los Angeles in 2016. For the record, the Raiders have moved twice, and another move—this one from Oakland to Las Vegas—has been approved by the league and will take place in 2020.

5. Carolina and Jacksonville

6. 1-C, 2-D, 3-F, 4-I, 5-G, 6-B, 7-H, 8-E, 9-A

7. D—On October 17, 1976, the two teams combined to play a game that had 39 penalties—35 of them accepted, two off-setting, and two declined—for a total of 310 penalty yards. It included 16 holding penalties, and twice Tampa Bay was called for having 12 men on the field.

8. A—As a team, New England finished with 3,165 rushing yards that season, a mark that still stands.

9. D—Philadelphia rushed for just 298 yards that season, an 11-game campaign.

10. B—Peyton Manning and the 2013 Broncos had the most prolific single-season passing attack in league history with 5,444 net passing yards.

11. D—That Kansas City team finished the year with 1,660 net passing yards that year; for quarterbacks Steve Fuller and Mike Livingston, it was a woeful average of 104 passing yards per game for a team that finished 7–9.

12. The Redskins and Giants in a 1966 game. Washington won the game, 72–41. The resulting 72–41 score is also the highest aggregate score in NFL history.

13. 1-H, 2-I, 3-J, 4-F, 5-B, 6-C, 7-D, 8-G, 9-A, 10-E

14. A—The Cardinals, who went from 1947 to 1998 without a playoff win.

15. B—That year, Baltimore went 2–3 in that run, but only lost one other game all season, setting an NFL record with 165 points allowed.

NAME GAME

1. Raiders at Colts. A divisional playoff game between Oakland and Baltimore on December 24, 1977, turned on a deep ball from Ken Stabler to Dave Casper. The 42-yard pass, coming in the final moments of regulation, paved the way for a game-tying field goal for the Raiders. Oakland eventually won it in double overtime.

2. Raiders at Patriots. This divisional playoff showdown, the last game played at Foxboro Stadium, was a tightly-contested affair that was played in a winter storm in January 2002. Also known as the "Tuck Rule Game" because of an officiating decision, a pair of clutch field goals helped lift New England to the 16–13 win.

3. Cowboys at Packers. The 1967 NFL championship between Dallas and Green Bay was played in blisteringly cold temperatures that dipped to 13 below. In a dramatic finish, Packers quarterback Bart Starr delivered on a quarterback sneak late in the game to allow Green Bay to upend the Cowboys and come away with the title.

4. Eagles at Bears. A 1988 NFC divisional playoff showdown between Philly and Chicago that was supposed to be remembered as a clash between rival coaches Mike Ditka and Buddy Ryan became one of the more memorable weather games in NFL history. A thick fog rolled in midway through the first half, making it almost impossible to see the game from the sidelines. The Bears won, 20–12.

5. Raiders at Steelers. Another dramatic playoff finish, this one involved Oakland and Pittsburgh in 1972. With the Steelers driving late in the game, Terry Bradshaw flung it deep downfield, but the ball took a crazy bounce after running back Frenchy Fuqua—the intended target—was hit. However, Franco Harris was trailing the play at the Raiders' 42, picked the ball out of the air at his shoe tops, and took off down the sideline. Some

Oakland players gave chase, but they couldn't stop Harris from scoring and giving the Steelers the win.

6. Buffalo at Tennessee. This January 8, 2000, playoff game is one of the more dramatic in recent league history. The Bills held a narrow fourth-quarter lead—16–15—but after Buffalo kicked off to the Titans as the clock ticked toward zero, Tennessee used a timely lateral to score a late touchdown, with wide receiver Kevin Dyson crossing the goal line to give the Titans the win.

7. Denver at Cleveland. John Elway led the Broncos on a 98-yard drive at the end of regulation in the 1986 AFC championship game to tie the game and break the hearts of Browns fans everywhere. Denver ended up winning the game in overtime on a 38-yard field goal and going to the Super Bowl.

8. New Orleans at Minnesota. Stefon Diggs scored on a 61-yard touchdown pass from Case Keenum as time ran out to give the Vikings a win in the 2017 NFC division playoff contest against the Saints.

9. The Colts and Giants in the 1958 NFL Championship, a game where Baltimore dramatically upended New York, 23–17.

10. The 2003 NFC divisional playoff game between the Packers and the Eagles. With 1:12 left in regulation and Philly trailing Green Bay, the Eagles faced a 4th-and-26, but Donovan McNabb hit Freddie Mitchell on a slant to pick up the first down. The play set up a field goal forcing overtime, in which the Eagles pulled out the 20–17 victory.

LOGO LOGIC

1. C—Rams. In 1948, Fred Gehrke, a player for the Rams who had studied art in college, came up with the idea of painting horns on the sides of the helmets. The idea was a hit, and other teams soon copied the idea.

2. C—Steelers. Owner Art Rooney gave a directive to longtime Pittsburgh equipment manager Jack Hart to do this to see how the logo would look on the gold helmets; however, its popularity led the team to leave it that way permanently.

3. B—He came to be known as Bucco Bruce.

4. Thirteen—Cardinals, Falcons, Ravens, Bills, Panthers, Broncos, Lions, Texans, Dolphins, Eagles, Seahawks, Rams, and Jaguars.

5. Six—Bears, Packers, Niners, Giants, Titans, and Chiefs.

6. Four—Patriots, Raiders, Redskins, and Bucs.

7. Seven—Browns, Cowboys, Colts, Saints, Steelers, Chargers, and Jets.

8. A—Ford initially believed the proposed Jaguars logo bore too much resemblance to its logo. It never reached the inside of a courtroom, but lawyers from the team and the auto maker negotiated an ultimately amicable agreement whereby Jaguar would be named the official car of the Jaguars, and the Jaguars would redesign their logo.

9. C—The Chargers' powder-blue uniforms, which are worn occasionally by the franchise these days, harken back to the classic uniforms the team wore in the 1960s and 1970s.

10. D—The Colts have moved from Baltimore to Indianapolis, but the logo and helmet have fundamentally remained the same since 1957, with only minor changes to the facemask, but for the most part, they've had the same logo, the same colors, and the same general look.

NICKNAME NONSENSE

1. 1-D, 2-F, 3-G, 4-A, 5-H, 6-B, 7-O, 8-C, 9-E, 10-Q, 11-I, 12-P, 13-J, 14-N, 15-K, 16-L, 17-M

POSTSEASON

QUESTIONS

"This is why you lift all them weights! This is why you do all that (bleep)!"
 —*Bill Parcells, caught by NFL Films exhorting his Giants team during a key playoff moment.*

The playoffs are where legends are made, where average players can become stars, and where great players can transcend the game and achieve epic status. For many, it's also a place where careers can rise and fall on one play. David Tyree, who was relatively anonymous before Super Bowl XLII, doesn't have to buy a drink the rest of his life when he walks into a bar in the Greater New York area. Meanwhile, Scott Norwood is still coming to grips with his miss in Super Bowl XXV against the Giants. In the end, the playoffs remain the ultimate test of mental and physical toughness as teams are winnowed on the road to the ultimate showdown.

1. Which one of these players is *not* on the top 5 list of all-time postseason games played in a career?
A. Brett Favre
B. Jerry Rice

C. Tom Brady
D. Adam Vinatieri
Answer on page 195.

2. The two quarterbacks to beat Tom Brady and Peyton Manning in the same postseason were:
A. Russell Wilson and Philip Rivers
B. Ben Roethlisberger and Aaron Rodgers
C. Joe Flacco and Mark Sanchez
D. Jake Plummer and Tony Romo
Answer on page 195.

3. Who is the only quarterback in the top 10 in career play-off passing yards *not* to win a Super Bowl?
A. Donovan McNabb
B. Matt Hasselbeck
C. Dan Marino
D. Warren Moon
Answer on page 195.

4. Tom Brady is tops on the career playoff passing list with 11,179 yards. Who is the only other active quarterback currently in the all-time top 5?
A. Drew Brees
B. Aaron Rodgers
C. Joe Flacco
D. Ben Roethlisberger
Answer on page 195.

5. Four current or former Patriots are in the top 20 when it comes to career playoff receiving yardage. Who are they?
A. Julian Edelman

B. Rob Gronkowski
C. Randy Moss
D. Deion Branch
Answer on page 195.

6. Who is the only running back in the top 5 in career play-off rushing yards not to win a Super Bowl?
   A. Earnest Byner
   B. Thurman Thomas
   C. Curtis Martin
   D. Chuck Foreman
   Answer on page 195.

7. True or False: Eric Dickerson holds the single-game play-off rushing record.
   Answer on page 195.

8. Which team has the longest current playoff drought when you count appearances?
   A. Browns
   B. Bucs
   C. Jets
   D. Niners
   Answer on page 195.

9. Which coach got his teams to the playoffs 19 times, an NFL mark?
   A. Bill Belichick
   B. Paul Brown
   C. Don Shula
   D. Tom Landry
   Answer on page 195.

10. This Niners' pass catcher was on the receiving end of one of the most memorable playoff touchdowns of all time, a last-minute heave from Joe Montana in the 1981 NFC title game against the Cowboys.
A. Dwight Clark
B. Russ Francis
C. Vernon Davis
D. John Taylor
Answer on page 196.

11. Which Dallas quarterback is credited with popularizing the term "Hail Mary" when it comes to late touchdown passes following a big play in the final moments of a post-season win over the Vikings?
A. Troy Aikman
B. Roger Staubach
C. Clint Stoerner
D. Quincy Carter
Answer on page 196.

12. Who is the only tight end who has 10 or more career playoff touchdowns?
A. Rob Gronkowski
B. Tony Gonzalez
C. Kellen Winslow
D. Mike Ditka
Answer on page 196.

13. Which one of these players never reached the postseason in their NFL career?
A. Vinny Testaverde
B. Junior Seau

C. Brandon Tyrone Marshall (WR)
D. Cris Carter
Answer on page 196.

14. Who were the quarterback and receiver on the famous "Sea of Hands" play at the end of the 1974 Oakland-Miami divisional playoff game?
Answer on page 196.

15. Name the only team to reach both the AFC and NFC title games.
Answer on page 196.

16. In NFL history, four teams made the playoffs with losing records. Who were they?
Answer on page 196.

17. Two players who played the bulk of their postseason careers with the same team are 1–2 when it comes to career playoff scoring. Who are they and what franchise is it?
Answer on page 196.

18. Since 1982—the first-year sacks were tallied as an official statistic by the NFL—who is tops when it comes to most career playoff sacks?
A. Reggie White
B. James Harrison
C. Dwight Freeney
D. Willie McGinest
Answer on page 196.

19. Which offensive player has the most career playoff games under his belt?
A. Jerry Rice
B. Peyton Manning
C. Tom Brady
D. Ben Roethlisberger
Answer on page 196.

20. Which quarterback has taken the most career playoff sacks?
A. Peyton Manning
B. Joe Montana
C. Troy Aikman
D. Tom Brady
Answer on page 197.

21. Which defensive player has the most career playoff games under his belt?
A. Willie McGinest
B. D. D. Lewis
C. Bill Romanowski
D. Charles Haley
Answer on page 197.

22. Which four players are tied at the top of the all-time list for most career postseason interceptions?
Answer on page 197.

23. Who has the playoff record for most non-offensive touchdowns?
A. Ed Reed
B. Asante Samuel

C. D. D. Lewis

D. Willie Brown

Answer on page 197.

24. Which six quarterbacks who have started at least 10 play-off games have a winning percentage of .700 or better?
Answer on page 197.

25. Which four quarterbacks have lost 10 or more playoff games?
Answer on page 197.

GOAT HORNS

The playoffs present an environment in which the pressure can make or break people. Many of these guys had terrific careers in the NFL, but for whatever reason, failed to execute in a big postseason moment. Below is the player in question. Describe their postseason gaffe.

1. Gary Anderson.
Answer on page 197.

2. Mike Vanderjagt.
Answer on page 197.

3. Blair Walsh.
Answer on page 197.

4. Tony Romo.
Answer on page 198.

5. Trey Junkin.
Answer on page 198.

6. Earnest Byner.
Answer on page 198.

7. Brian Sipe.
Answer on page 198.

8. Cody Parkey.
Answer on page 198.

9. Brett Favre.
Answer on page 198.

10. Rahim Moore.
Answer on page 198.

11. Roger Craig.
Answer on page 198.

UNDER-THE-RADAR STARS

When it comes to clutch performances in the playoffs, it's not always the players you'd expect. This section pays tribute to some surprise stars of the NFL playoffs. Below is the player's name. Identify the circumstances in which they delivered in the big moment.

1. Frank Reich.
Answer on page 199.

2. Sterling Moore.
Answer on page 199.

3. Don Strock.
Answer on page 199.

4. A. J. Duhe.
Answer on page 199.

5. Ricky Manning, Jr.
Answer on page 199.

6. Sam Shields.
Answer on page 200.

7. Tommy Maddox.
Answer on page 200.

POSTSEASON

ANSWERS

1. A—Favre played in 24 career postseason games, which is tied for 10th in NFL history. By way of comparison, Brady tops the list with 40.

2. C—Sanchez did it in 2010, and Flacco did it in 2012.

3. C—Marino has 4,510 postseason passing yards, good for eighth on the all-time list.

4. D—Roethlisberger is fifth overall with 5,256 career playoff passing yards.

5. Julian Edelman, Rob Gronkowski, Randy Moss, Deion Branch.

6. B—Thomas is third all-time in career playoff rushing yards with 1,442.

7. True—Dickerson rushed for 248 yards in a Rams 20–0 playoff win over the Cowboys in January 1986.

8. A—Cleveland's last playoff appearance was 2002.

9. C—Shula did it with the Colts and Dolphins.

10. A—Clark was the one who came down with "The Catch" to help lift San Francisco past Dallas and into the Super Bowl.

11. B—It was Staubach who lofted a deep ball for Drew Pearson in the final seconds of a 1975 divisional playoff game against Minnesota that lifted the Cowboys to victory. After the game, Staubach was asked what happened. "I just threw the ball as far as I could and said a Hail Mary," he replied.

12. A—Gronkowski has 12 career postseason touchdowns, tied for sixth on the all-time list among players at any position.

13. C—As of 2018, Marshall had played in 178 regular-season games without having appeared in the playoffs during his 13-season career.

14. Ken Stabler and Clarence Davis.

15. Seattle. The Seahawks were part of the AFC from 1977 until 2001, then switched to the NFC. In 1983, they lost the AFC championship game to the Raiders; they won NFC titles in 2005 and 2014, and won it all in 2013.

16. In the strike-shortened 1982 season—with teams limited to nine games—the Browns and Lions both made it with 4–5 records. In 2010, the 7–9 Seahawks won the woeful NFC West. And in 2014, Carolina landed in the playoffs with a woeful 7–8–1 mark.

17. Adam Vinatieri and Stephen Gostkowski, both of the New England Patriots.

18. D—McGinest finished his playing career with 16 postseason sacks.

19. C—Brady has played in 40 playoff games in his career.

20. D—Brady has been sacked 66 times in the postseason over the course of his career. For the record, Brady also holds the all-time record for most postseason interceptions with 34.

21. B—Lewis was a linebacker who played in 27 career postseason games as a member of the Cowboys.

22. Ronnie Lott, Ed Reed, Charlie Waters, and Bill Simpson.

23. B—Samuel, a cornerback with the Patriots, Eagles, and Falcons, had four postseason touchdowns—three with New England and one with Philadelphia.

24. Bart Starr 9–1 (.900); Jim Plunkett 8–2 (.800); Tom Brady 30–10 (.750); Otto Graham (.750); Terry Bradshaw 14–5 (.737); Troy Aikman 11–4 (.733).

25. Peyton Manning 13; Brett Favre 11; Dan Marino 10; Tom Brady 10.

GOAT HORNS

1. The Vikings kicker missed a 39-yarder late in the 1998 NFC championship game—his first miss after connecting on 35 straight field-goal attempts in the regular season—that would have secured the victory for Minnesota and sent the Vikings to the Super Bowl. Instead, Anderson's miss paved the way for an Atlanta comeback.

2. The Colts kicker missed a 46-yarder with 21 seconds left in the 2006 AFC divisional round against the Steelers, allowing Pittsburgh to come away with the dramatic win.

3. The Vikings kicker missed a 27-yarder with 26 seconds left in regulation to give Seattle a 10–9 wild-card win in the 2016 postseason.

4. In a 2006 NFC wild-card game against the Seahawks, the Cowboys quarterback bobbled the snap on what would have been a chip-shot field goal to win the game. He recovered the ball and attempted to run it in, but was tackled short of the first-down marker, and Dallas lost, 21–20.

5. Another botched playoff snap with the season on the line. The veteran long snapper failed to deliver the ball cleanly late in a 2002 wild-card game against the Niners, and the Giants suffered a last-second defeat.

6. Byner's goal-line fumble late in the 1987 AFC championship game against the Broncos left the Browns deflated, as Denver went to the Super Bowl.

7. The Cleveland quarterback—who was the league MVP that season—was leading the Browns to what would have almost certainly been a game-winning score in a 1980 divisional playoff showdown against the Raiders, but threw a late interception that sealed the loss.

8. The Chicago kicker missed a 43-yard field goal attempt at the end of a 2018 wild-card playoff game against the Eagles, ending the Bears' season.

9. With the game tied at 28, the Vikings' veteran threw an ill-advised interception late in regulation of the 2009 NFC title game against the Saints. New Orleans took advantage, scoring in overtime to advance to the Super Bowl.

10. In a 2012 divisional playoff showdown with the Ravens, the Broncos safety allowed Baltimore receiver Jacoby Jones to get behind him and score on a late 70-yard touchdown pass that helped the Ravens advance to the AFC title game.

11. With San Francisco holding a 13–12 lead late in the 1990 NFC title showdown with the New York Giants and looking to run out the clock, the usually reliable Niners veteran fumbled. The ball went back to the Giants, and a late field goal from Matt Bahr won the game for New York.

UNDER-THE-RADAR STARS

1. Thrust into the spotlight after an injury to starter Jim Kelly in the 1992 playoffs, the Bills' backup quarterback was facing an uphill climb against the Oilers—Buffalo trailed 35–3 at halftime. But Reich rallied the Bills, throwing 21 of his 34 passes for 289 yards and four touchdowns on his way to a comeback. The Bills won the game in overtime, 41–38.

2. A backup cornerback on New England's 2011 team, he found himself in coverage against Baltimore receiver Lee Evans late in the AFC title contest. On a pass to the end zone from Joe Flacco, Moore knocked the ball away, preventing what would have almost surely been a game-winning touchdown. The Patriots went on to win the game and advance to the Super Bowl.

3. The backup quarterback came off the bench in the second half of Miami's divisional playoff contest against the Chargers on January 2, 1982, and led Miami from a 24–0 deficit to tie the score in the third quarter. Ultimately, Miami lost the game to San Diego, 41–38, in overtime.

4. Considered a good but not great player, in the 1982 AFC title game, he rose to the occasion against the Jets. A former defensive lineman who converted to linebacker, Duhe intercepted Jets quarterback Richard Todd three times in a 14–0 win that gave the Dolphins an AFC championship.

5. The rookie corner had a good first season in the NFL with Carolina, but surprised many with his eye-popping performance in the postseason. He had four picks in the 2003 playoffs, including three in the NFC title game against Donovan McNabb and the Eagles.

6. The undrafted free agent had a pair of interceptions, a forced fumble, and a sack in Green Bay's 21–14 win over the Bears in the 2010 NFC title game.

7. The former XFL signal-caller took over for Pittsburgh's Kordell Stewart after he was injured early in a 2002 playoff contest, and proceeded to have the game of his life, throwing three touchdown passes during the final 19 minutes as the Steelers stormed back for a 36–33 win. He finished 30 of 48 for 367 yards.

QUESTIONS

"If it's the ultimate game, how come they're playing it again next year?"
—*Cowboys running back Duane Thomas*
before Super Bowl VI

"If you've ever won a championship, then that's all you're interested in doing."
—*Bill Parcells*

When the AFL and NFL joined to create one league, they were stumped to come up with a name for their championship contest. One suggestion was the "World Series of Football." Another wanted to call the game simply "The Big One." Commissioner Pete Rozelle suggested "The AFL-NFL Championship Game." While Rozelle's suggestion was technically accurate, it lacked pizazz needed to sell the contest, not to mention the fact that newspapers would have a problem squeezing it into a headline. Turns out, Chiefs owner Lamar Hunt had a winner. His son, Lamar, Jr., tells the story:

My dad was in an owners meeting. They were trying to figure out what to call the last game, the championship game. I don't know if he had the ball with him as some reports suggest. My dad said, "Well, we need to come up with a name, something like the 'Super

Bowl.'" And then he said, "Actually, that's not a very good name. We can come up with something better." But "Super Bowl" stuck.

1. True or False: Bart Starr was the first Super Bowl MVP.
   Answer on page 217.

2. Who was the first non-quarterback to win the Super Bowl MVP?
   Answer on page 217.

3. Which Super Bowl record does Tom Brady *not* hold?
   A. Game Passer Rating
   B. Game Passing Yards
   C. Game Passes Completed
   D. Career Passing Leader
   Answer on page 217.

4. Which three teams have a point differential better than plus-50 in the Super Bowl (minimum of five Super Bowl appearances)?
   A. New England, Pittsburgh, San Francisco
   B. San Francisco, Dallas, Green Bay
   C. Green Bay, Pittsburgh, Oakland/Los Angeles
   D. Washington, Oakland/Los Angeles, New York Giants
   Answer on page 217.

5. _____ scored the first points in the history of the Super Bowl, and what was the play?
   Answer on page 217.

6. Which two NFL teams are tied with the most Super Bowl losses—five?

A. Patriots, Vikings
B. Patriots, Broncos
C. Patriots, Raiders
D. Patriots, Bills
Answer on page 217.

7. True or false: The Ravens' Jacoby Jones's 108-yard kick return for a touchdown against the 49ers in Super Bowl XLVII is the longest play in Super Bowl history.
Answer on page 217.

8. Who was the oldest player to take part in a Super Bowl?
A. Tom Brady
B. Shane Lechler
C. Sean Jones
D. Matt Stover
Answer on page 217.

9. Who was the youngest player to take part in a Super Bowl?
A. Tom Brady
B. Jamal Lewis
C. Bart Starr
D. Jack Ham
Answer on page 217.

10. What was the one year the Super Bowl was officially referred to without roman numerals?
A. Super Bowl I
B. Super Bowl X
C. Super Bowl L
D. None. It has always used roman numerals
Answer on page 217.

11. Which team has the most Super Bowl MVPs?
A. Patriots
B. Packers
C. Steelers
D. Cowboys
Answer on page 218.

12. Which of these wide receivers did *not* win a Super Bowl MVP award?
A. Hines Ward
B. John Stallworth
C. Fred Biletnikoff
D. Deion Branch
Answer on page 218.

13. True or False: The MVP has gone to a player on the losing team at least once.
Answer on page 218.

14. Name the four players who have won the Heisman and Super Bowl MVP.
Answer on page 218.

15. Which one of these positions has *never* produced a Super Bowl MVP?
A. Defensive back
B. Linebacker
C. Tight end
D. Running back
Answer on page 218.

16. The three players who are tied for the most individual Super Bowl losses all got four of them with the same team. Name that team.
A. Denver
B. Buffalo
C. Minnesota
D. San Diego
Answer on page 218.

17. In addition to tying the individual mark for most career Super Bowl losses, which player has appeared in the most consecutive Super Bowls?
A. Craig Morton
B. John Elway
C. Jim Kelly
D. Gale Gilbert
Answer on page 218.

18. How many first-quarter points have the Patriots scored in their nine Super Bowl appearances since 2001?
A. 0
B. 21
C. 14
D. 3
Answer on page 218.

19. True or False: Mean Joe Greene was the first player to win three straight Super Bowls.
Answer on page 218.

20. Three players have won a Super Bowl one year, and then returned to the Super Bowl the following year and beat their old team to go back-to-back as a part of different teams. Name them.
Answer on page 219.

21. Which Steelers running back holds the Super Bowl record for longest rush from scrimmage?
A. Franco Harris
B. Le'Veon Bell
C. Jerome Bettis
D. Willie Parker
Answer on page 219.

22. _____ has the Super Bowl record for most career yards from scrimmage.
Answer on page 219.

23. These two kickers are tied for most career field goals made in Super Bowl action.
A. Matt Bahr and Stephen Gostkowski
B. Stephen Gostkowski and Adam Vinatieri
C. Adam Vinatieri and Ray Wersching
D. Ray Wersching and Uwe Von Schamann
Answer on page 219.

24. Which Steeler tops the list of all-time Super Bowl sack leaders?
A. Joe Greene
B. James Harrison
C. L. C. Greenwood
D. Dwight White
Answer on page 219.

25. Who was the quarterback and pass catcher on the longest pass play in Super Bowl history?
A. Tom Brady and Rob Gronkowski
B. Jake Delhomme and Muhsin Muhammad
C. Dan Marino and Mark Clayton
D. Bart Starr and Max McGee
Answer on page 219.

26. This quarterback has thrown the most career interceptions in the big game.
A. Jim Kelly
B. Fran Tarkenton
C. John Elway
D. Tom Brady
Answer on page 219.

27. _____ was the first player to utter these words after a Super Bowl win: "I'm going to Disney World!"
Answer on page 219.

28. This kicker drilled the longest field goal in Super Bowl history.
A. Adam Vinatieri
B. Steve Christie
C. Kevin Butler
D. Mike Vanderjagt
Answer on page 219.

29. Which non-kicker has scored the most career points in Super Bowl history?
A. Jerry Rice
B. Emmitt Smith
C. Franco Harris
D. Roger Craig
Answer on page 219.

30. True or False: Emmitt Smith is among the players who are tied at the top (three) with most touchdowns in a single Super Bowl.
Answer on page 219.

31. Which Steelers linebacker threw an opponent to the turf during a Super Bowl because an opponent patted the Pittsburgh kicker on the head condescendingly after a missed field-goal attempt?
A. James Harrison
B. Jack Lambert
C. Joey Porter
D. Jack Ham
Answer on page 219.

32. James Harrison executed what memorable play in Super Bowl XLIII?
Answer on page 220.

33. Of the teams that have won multiple Super Bowls, which franchise still has a point differential of more than minus-100 when it comes to Super Bowl play?
A. New England
B. Denver
C. Los Angeles

D. Miami
Answer on page 220.

34. As of 2019, 12 teams haven't won the Super Bowl. Name them.
Answer on page 220.

35. How many NFL teams have hosted a Super Bowl in their own stadium?
Answer on page 220.

36. Through the 2018 season, which two cities have hosted the most Super Bowls?
Answer on page 220.

37. Who had the ball and who made the tackle on the last play of Super Bowl XXXIV between St. Louis and Tennessee?
Answer on page 220.

38. Who was Russell Wilson's intended target on the pass that was picked off by Malcolm Butler near the end of Super Bowl XLIX?
A. Doug Baldwin
B. Ricardo Lockett
C. Jermaine Kearse
D. Chris Matthews
Answer on page 220.

39. Which school has produced the most Super Bowl MVPs?
A. Southern Cal
B. Notre Dame
C. Nebraska
D. Michigan
Answer on page 220.

40. Which team has four or more Super Bowl losses, but never led for a single second of any of those four defeats?
A. Buffalo
B. Denver
C. Minnesota
D. New England
Answer on page 221.

DECONSTRUCTING THE DYNASTIES

While the NFL boasts of parity, with a salary cap, balanced sched-uling, and all the other elements designed to keep all 32 teams on an even playing field, there are a handful of teams who have con-sistently managed to rise above and become the toast of the league. In all, six teams have won 30 of the 53 Super Bowls—at least four each. In this section, we focus on the NFL's dynasties: New England, Pittsburgh, San Francisco, Dallas, Green Bay, and the New York Giants—and their most memorable Super Bowl moments.

New England

1. Who scored the first points in Super Bowl action for the Patriots?
A. Troy Brown
B. Tony Franklin
C. Ben Coates
D. Craig James
Answer on page 221.

2. Name the four offensive skill position players for New England who are among the top seven in most receptions in a single Super Bowl contest.
Answer on page 221.

3. Who is the only player in franchise history to record at least one sack and one touchdown in Super Bowl action?
A. Rodney Harrison
B. Mike Vrabel
C. Troy Brown
D. Julian Edelman
Answer on page 221.

4. Which New England defender has the franchise record for most interceptions in Super Bowl action?
A. Darrelle Revis
B. Ty Law
C. Stephon Gilmore
D. Rodney Harrison
Answer on page 221.

Pittsburgh

1. Name the Steelers' Super Bowl MVPs.
Answer on page 221.

2. Which Pittsburgh quarterback leads the franchise when it comes to passing touchdowns in Super Bowl action?
Answer on page 221.

3. True or False: Mean Joe Greene leads the franchise with the most Super Bowl sacks.
Answer on page 221.

4. Who scored the Steelers' first points in Super Bowl competition?
A. Lynn Swann
B. Franco Harris
C. Dwight White
D. Terry Bradshaw
Answer on page 221.

San Francisco

1. Which Niners quarterback has the Super Bowl record for most touchdown passes in a game?
A. Steve Young
B. Joe Montana
C. Steve Bono
D. Colin Kaepernick
Answer on page 222.

2. Three Niners are tied with Denver's Terrell Davis and New England's James White for most touchdowns in one Super Bowl game with three. Who are they?
Answer on page 222.

3. True or false: The Niners have the largest point differential of any team in Super Bowl action.
Answer on page 222.

4. Which Super Bowl involving the Niners saw a portion of the lights go out in the second half?
Answer on page 222.

Dallas

1. The Cowboys have had seven players win Super Bowl MVP awards, more than any other team. Name the only Dallas cornerback to win the honor.
   Answer on page 222.

2. Which Cowboy had his helmet stolen immediately following Super Bowl XXVIII?
   A. Troy Aikman
   B. Michael Irvin
   C. Emmitt Smith
   D. Nate Newton
   Answer on page 222.

3. Name the Dallas quarterback who has thrown for the most yards in Super Bowl action.
   Answer on page 222.

4. Who was the Cowboy who dropped a sure touchdown pass in Super Bowl XIII?
   A. Jackie Smith
   B. Jason Witten
   C. Butch Johnson
   D. Preston Pearson
   Answer on page 222.

Green Bay

1. Brett Favre and Bart Starr each appeared in two Super Bowls. Who has the better overall passer rating in Super Bowl action?
   Answer on page 222.

2. Which Packer holds the franchise record for most career touchdowns in Super Bowl action?
A. Brett Favre
B. Max McGee
C. Antonio Freeman
D. Desmond Howard
Answer on page 222.

3. _____ was the only special teams player in Super Bowl history to win MVP honors for his performance against the Patriots in Super Bowl XXXI.
Answer on page 222.

4. Which Packers defender had three sacks in Super Bowl XXXI against the Patriots?
Answer on page 222.

New York

1. This receiver made a big catch late in the Super Bowl XLVI win over the Patriots.
A. David Tyree
B. Mario Manningham
C. Stephen Baker
D. Phil McConkey
Answer on page 223.

2. Who has more sacks in the Super Bowl—Michael Strahan or Lawrence Taylor?
Answer on page 223.

3. Which one of the four Giants quarterbacks who have started a Super Bowl has thrown the most career Super Bowl interceptions?
   A. Phil Simms
   B. Jeff Hostetler
   C. Kerry Collins
   D. Eli Manning
   Answer on page 223.

4. In addition to knocking off the Patriots and derailing the perfect season, what other distinction does the 2007 Giants' Super Bowl team hold?
   A. They were one of six wild-card teams to win a Super Bowl.
   B. Their run-pass splits in the postseason were a perfect 50–50.
   C. They had four different starting quarterbacks.
   D. They were the last team to wear blue jerseys to win a Super Bowl.
   Answer on page 223.

SUPER BOWL

ANSWERS

1. True—The Green Bay quarterback won the MVPs for the first two Super Bowls.

2. Linebacker Chuck Howley of the Cowboys won it in Super Bowl V.

3. A—Phil Simms holds the Super Bowl record for Game Passer Rating.

4. B—San Francisco, Dallas, and Green Bay.

5. The first points scored in Super Bowl I were on a 37-yard touchdown pass in the first quarter from Bart Starr to Max McGee.

6. B—Patriots and Broncos

7. True

8. D—Stover was 42 years and 11 days in Super Bowl XLIV; he was part of a Colts team that lost to the Saints.

9. B—Lewis was 21 years and 152 days when he was part of a Baltimore team that beat the Giants in Super Bowl XXXV.

10. C—It was referred to by the league as Super Bowl 50.

11. D—Cowboys, who have had seven: Chuck Howley, Roger Staubach, Harvey Martin, Randy White, Troy Aikman, Emmitt Smith, Larry Brown.

12. B—Stallworth was a part of four Super Bowl winners in Pittsburgh, but never won a Super Bowl MVP award.

13. True—Dallas linebacker Chuck Howley won the award for his performance in a losing effort in Super Bowl V. He intercepted two passes and forced a fumble, but Dallas lost to Baltimore.

14. Roger Staubach—Navy, Cowboys; Jim Plunkett—Stanford, Raiders; Marcus Allen—Southern Cal, Raiders; Desmond Howard—Michigan, Packers.

15. C—No tight end has ever won a Super Bowl MVP award.

16. B—Glenn Parker, Cornelius Bennett, and Gale Gilbert were all part of Buffalo's teams that lost four straight Super Bowls. Parker suffered his fifth loss with the Giants in Super Bowl XXXV, while Bennett and the Falcons lost in Super Bowl XXXIII and Gilbert was part of the San Diego team that lost at the hands of the Niners in Super Bowl XXIX.

17. D—Gilbert appeared in five straight consecutive Super Bowls, which is an individual mark. He appeared in four with the Bills and one with the Chargers.

18. D—Despite having some of the highest-scoring offenses in recent league history, the Patriots have only scored three points in the first quarter in their nine Super Bowl appearances involving Brady and Belichick.

19. False. Linebacker Ken Norton, Jr. won three straight as a member of the Cowboys and Niners in the early 1990s.

20. Brandon Browner, who went from the Seahawks to the Patriots between Super Bowl XLVIII and XLIX and Chris Long and LeGarrette Blount, who went from the Patriots to the Eagles between Super Bowl LI and LII.

21. D—Parker ran for 75 yards on one play in Super Bowl XL against the Seahawks.

22. In four games, Jerry Rice has 604 career yards in Super Bowl action.

23. B—Gostkowski and Vinatieri are tied with seven each.

24. C—Greenwood has five career Super Bowl sacks.

25. B—Delhomme and Muhammad connected on an 85-yard pass play for a touchdown against the Patriots in Super Bowl XXXVIII.

26. C—Elway. The former Denver quarterback has thrown eight interceptions in five career Super Bowl games.

27. Phil Simms was the first player to take part in the promotion; he was MVP of Super Bowl XXI.

28. B—The Bills' Christie hit a 54-yard field goal in Super Bowl XXVIII against Dallas.

29. A—Rice. The former Niners receiver has scored 48 career points in Super Bowl action.

30. False. Smith scored two touchdowns in Super Bowl XXX and XXVIII, but never three in a game. For what it's worth, Smith has the most career rushing touchdowns in Super Bowl action with five.

31. B—Lambert saw Dallas' Cliff Harris try and torment kicker Roy Gerela after Gerela missed a field goal in Super Bowl X, and he tossed Harris angrily to the ground.

32. Intercepted Arizona quarterback Kurt Warner and took it back 100 yards for a memorable pick-six in the Steelers' win over the Cardinals.

33. B—In their history, the Broncos have gone 2–3 in the Super Bowl, but they're still -112 when it comes to point differential in Super Bowl play. New England is second in that group at minus-36.

34. The Bengals, Bills, Browns, Cardinals, Chargers, Falcons, Jaguars, Lions, Panthers, Texans, Titans, and Vikings have not won a Super Bowl in their history. For what it's worth, the Browns, Jaguars, Lions, and Texans have not reached the Super Bowl.

35. None, although two teams have reached the Super Bowl hosted in their home *region*: the San Francisco 49ers, who played Super Bowl XIX in Stanford Stadium, rather than Candlestick Park, and the Los Angeles Rams, who played Super Bowl XIV in the Rose Bowl, rather than the Los Angeles Memorial Coliseum.

36. Miami and New Orleans have each hosted 10. In February 2020, Miami will break that tie, as it is set to host Super Bowl LIV.

37. Kevin Dyson had the ball for the Titans and was tackled a yard shy of the goal line by Rams linebacker Mike Jones.

38. B—Wilson threw to Lockett, but Butler intercepted the ball, allowing New England to come away with the dramatic win.

39. D—Michigan has produced five Super Bowl MVPs—Tom Brady has won four, while Desmond Howard has one of his own. Alabama, Georgia, Notre Dame, and USC each have three.

40. C—Minnesota was on the losing end of Super Bowls IV, VIII, IX, and XI. The Vikings didn't lead in any of those games.

DECONSTRUCTING THE DYNASTIES

New England

1. B—The kicker banged home a 36-yard field goal in the first quarter of Super Bowl XX to give the Patriots a short-lived 3–0 lead.

2. James White, Shane Vereen, Wes Welker, and Deion Branch.

3. B—Vrabel has three sacks in the four Super Bowls he took part in and added a touchdown while lining up as a tight end in Super Bowl XXXIX against the Eagles.

4. D—Harrison had two picks in Super Bowl action, both of them in Super Bowl XXXIX against Philadelphia.

Pittsburgh

1. Terry Bradshaw has won twice, while Lynn Swann, Franco Harris, Hines Ward, and Santonio Holmes have each won one.

2. Bradshaw has nine touchdown passes, while Ben Roethlisberger has three in three Super Bowl appearances.

3. False: L. C. Greenwood had five career Super Bowl sacks, an NFL record. Four of those came in Super Bowl X.

4. C—White gave the Steelers an early 2–0 lead with a safety on the way to a 16–6 victory in Super Bowl IX over Minnesota.

San Francisco

1. A—Young threw six touchdown passes in Super Bowl XXIX against the Chargers.

2. Jerry Rice—who did it twice—as well as Ricky Watters and Roger Craig.

3. True. In its six Super Bowl appearances, San Francisco has outscored the opposition by a combined 96 points, best in the league.

4. Super Bowl XLVII

Dallas

1. Larry Brown, who had two interceptions in Super Bowl XXX. He became the first cornerback to take home the award.

2. C—Smith. The future all-time leading rusher had his helmet taken by someone during the postgame celebration. It was found a couple of days later.

3. Roger Staubach threw for 734 yards in four Super Bowl games. Troy Aikman had 689 in three Super Bowl contests.

4. A—Smith

Green Bay

1. Starr. He had a 106 passer rating in his two Super Bowl starts for the Packers.

2. C—Freeman has three Super Bowl touchdowns to his credit—one in Super Bowl XXXI and two in Super Bowl XXXII.

3. Desmond Howard

4. Reggie White

New York

1. B—Manningham connected with Eli Manning on a reception down the sideline late in the fourth quarter—a 38-yarder that was the longest play from scrimmage in the game.

2. Strahan. He's credited with 2.5 sacks in his two Super Bowls, while Taylor never registered a sack in either of his Super Bowls.

3. C—Collins threw four interceptions, all in a Super Bowl XXXV loss to the Ravens.

4. A—The 2007 Giants were one of six wild-card teams to win it all.

HALL OF FAME

QUESTIONS

"At night, there's a time when [the fans] all leave . . . I believe that the busts talk to each other. I can't wait for that conversation, I really can't. Vince Lombardi, Knute Rockne, Reggie, Walter Payton, all my ex-players, we'll be there forever and ever and ever talking about whatever. That's what I believe. That's what I think is going to happen, and no one's ever going to talk me out of that."
—John Madden on the Hall of Fame, 2006

With the NFL continuing to expand throughout the 1950s and '60s, the league decided it needed to have a Hall of Fame, and when they started looking for a location, Canton, Ohio, seemed like a natural fit. The reasons: Pro football could trace its roots back to Canton—that's where the first league was organized, and it was home to one of the first legendary teams, the Canton Bulldogs. They broke ground on the building in late 1962, and it opened its doors in Canton, Ohio on September 7, 1963. A modest start—two rooms and just 19,000 square feet of space—gave way to dreams of expansion, and in 1971 and 1977, the building added more square footage as tourists flocked to hear about the history of the game.

1. Which one of the following individuals was *not* part of the first class of inductees in 1963 at the Pro Football Hall of Fame?
A. George Halas
B. Sammy Baugh
C. Jim Thorpe
D. Otto Graham
Answer on page 233.

2. Which franchise is best represented in the Pro Football Hall of Fame?
A. Chicago
B. Oakland
C. Dallas
D. Philadelphia
Answer on page 233.

3. True or False: Johnny Unitas is the only member of the Pro Football Hall of Fame whose last name starts with the letter U.
Answer on page 233.

4. How many kickers are in the Hall of Fame?
A. None
B. One
C. Four
D. Ten
Answer on page 233.

5. Which one of these coaches is *not* in the Hall of Fame?
A. Mike Holmgren
B. Bud Grant

C. Weeb Ewbank

D. Marv Levy

Answer on page 233.

6. How many owners have been inducted into the Pro Football Hall of Fame as contributors?

Answer on page 233.

7. Who is the only person to be inducted into the Baseball Hall of Fame and Pro Football Hall of Fame?

A. Bo Jackson

B. Pete Rozelle

C. Cal Hubbard

D. Kirk Gibson

Answer on page 233.

8. Which position is best represented in the Hall of Fame?

A. Quarterbacks

B. Running backs

C. Wide receivers

D. Offensive linemen

Answer on page 233.

9. Of the position players who are in the Hall, which position has the fewest members represented?

A. Kickers

B. Defensive linemen

C. Punters

D. Fullbacks

Answer on page 234.

10. Eight schools have eight or more representatives in the Pro Football Hall of Fame. Name them.
Answer on page 234.

11. Of the players in the Hall of Fame, which uniform number is best represented among the enshrinees?
A. 12
B. 16
C. 22
D. 44
Answer on page 234.

12. Which four numbers have never been worn by a Hall of Fame player?
Answer on page 234.

13. Which Hall of Famer played the fewest total seasons but still managed to land a spot in Canton?
A. Terrell Davis
B. Doak Walker
C. Gayle Sayers
D. Ernie Nevers
Answer on page 234.

14. How many Hall of Famers have been taken first overall in the NFL draft?
Answer on page 234.

15. Using the draft rounds as a measure, which Hall of Fame player was drafted later than any other inductee?
A. Raymond Berry
B. Andy Robustelli

C. Roosevelt Brown
D. George Blanda
Answer on page 234.

16. Which foreign country has produced the most Hall of Famers?
    A. Canada
    B. Switzerland
    C. Spain
    D. Mexico
    Answer on page 234.

17. Who are the only three Hall of Famers to win multiple Super Bowl MVPs?
    Answer on page 234.

18. Four of the five youngest enshrinees had something in common. What was it?
    A. They were all running backs
    B. They were all sons of former players
    C. They were all part of the same class
    D. They all had the same last name
    Answer on page 234.

19. Who was the oldest Hall of Famer when he was enshrined?
    A. George Halas
    B. Ralph Wilson, Jr.
    C. Ed Sabol
    D. Hank Stram
    Answer on page 235.

20. Which future legend saw some of the first action of his career as a professional in the 2000 Hall of Fame preseason game?

A. Kurt Warner

B. Tom Brady

C. Jerome Bettis

D. Michael Strahan

Answer on page 235.

21. _____ was inducted into the Hall of Fame in 2006, becoming the first African-American quarterback and the first undrafted quarterback to receive the honor.

Answer on page 235.

22. Are there more coaches or quarterbacks in the Hall of Fame?

Answer on page 235.

23. Which Hall of Famer ran for the most regular-season touchdowns over the course of his career?

A. Marcus Allen

B. Walter Payton

C. Emmitt Smith

D. Jim Brown

Answer on page 235.

24. Which Hall of Famer holds the record for most regular-season games played by any defensive enshrinee?

A. Bruce Smith

B. Junior Seau

C. Darrell Green

D. Jason Taylor

Answer on page 235.

25. Name the four players in the Hall of Fame who played at least 300 regular-season games in their careers?
Answer on page 235.

HALL OF FAME

ANSWERS

1. D—Otto Graham

2. A—Chicago. Including the earliest incarnations of the franchise—the Decatur Staleys and Chicago Staleys—it has 33 members in the Hall.

3. False: Gene Upshaw and Brian Urlacher are the other two. There are two letters—I and Z—that are represented with just one inductee each, Michael Irvin and Gary Zimmerman.

4. C—Morten Andersen, Jan Stenrud, Lou Groza, and George Blanda. It's important to note Andersen and Stenrud were exclusively kickers, while Groza and Blanda also manned other positions.

5. A—Holmgren, who coached two teams to the Super Bowl—Green Bay and Seattle—has not been inducted into the Hall.

6. 16, including Denver's Pat Bowlen and Dallas' Jerry Jones.

7. C—Hubbard. He played in the NFL from 1927 to 1936 and later served as an umpire in Major League Baseball.

8. D—As of spring 2019, there were 46 offensive linemen in the Hall of Fame, more than any other position.

9. C—There's only one punter in the Pro Football Hall of Fame—Ray Guy. He was a member of the class of 2014.

10. Notre Dame (13); Southern California (12); Ohio State (10); Michigan (9); Alabama, Miami, Pittsburgh, and Syracuse (8).

11. C—According to the Hall of Fame's website, more inductees have worn the number 22 than any other set of digits. It's a group that includes "Bullet" Bob Hayes, Mike Haynes, and Bobby Layne.

12. 43, 69, 90, and 97.

13. D—Nevers played five seasons—two with the Duluth Eskimos from 1926–27, and three with the Chicago Cardinals from 1929–31. Nevers set what some consider to be an unbreakable record—playing for the Cardinals on November 28, 1929, Nevers scored every one of his team's points—six touchdowns and four extra point conversions—in a 40–6 win over the Chicago Bears.

14. 14, including the 1984 supplemental draft—It's a group that includes Terry Bradshaw, O. J. Simpson, Troy Aikman, Paul Hornung, John Elway, Earl Campbell, and Orlando Pace.

15. C—Brown was taken in the 27th round of the 1953 draft by the Giants. An offensive tackle out of Morgan State, he would go on to play 13 seasons and notch eight All-NFL selections.

16. A—Canada. Our neighbors to the north have produced two Hall of Famers, Bronko Nagurski and Arnie Weinmeister.

17. Joe Montana, Bart Starr, and Terry Bradshaw.

18. A—They were all running backs. Gayle Sayers was the youngest all-time inductee at the age of 34, Jim Brown and

Barry Sanders went in at the age of 35, and Earl Campbell was inducted at 36 years old.

19. C—Sabol, one of the founders of NFL Films, was 94 when he went in as part of the Class of 2011.

20. B—Brady was a backup that summer to Drew Bledsoe and saw mop-up duty in relief for the Patriots that evening. It was also the first preseason game for Bill Belichick as head coach for New England.

21. Warren Moon

22. Quarterbacks. There are 28 QBs and 23 coaches.

23. C—Smith had 164 career regular-season rushing touchdowns, more than any other Hall of Famer.

24. C—Green. The former Washington defensive back played 295 regular-season games over the course of his career, tops among all defensive players in the Hall of Fame.

25. Kicker Morten Andersen, quarterback/kicker George Blanda, wide receiver Jerry Rice, quarterback Brett Favre.